792.03
M 855c

Coming to Terms with Acting

An Instructive Glossary

WITHDRAWN

Doug Moston

D1314608

Drama Book Publishers
New York

© 1993 by Doug Moston
First Edition
All rights reserved under the International Pan-American
Copyright Conventions. For information address
Drama Book Publishers, 260 Fifth Avenue, New York,
New York 10001.

Library of Congress Cataloging in Publication Data

Moston, Doug
  Coming to terms with acting : an instructive glossary /
Doug Moston. - - 1st. ed.
  Includes bibliographical references.
  ISBN 0-89676-121-5 : $16.95
  1. Acting - - Dictionaries. I. Title.
PN2061.M67   1993
792'.03 - - dc20   93-4440
                                                      CIP

To my father, Murray, and my wife, Diana.

ALLEGHENY COLLEGE LIBRARY

Foreword

When I first heard about this book, I thought, "Why do we need another book on acting?" However, this is not just another book on acting and it is certainly much more than an ordinary glossary or concordance. It is not an absolute pronouncement of what the Method is or isn't, what Shakespeare was or is, or even the way to act. Rather, it is an attempt to broaden artistic choice by closing the gap between the differences of the language or jargon being used in the theatre today. Increasingly, classic terms and concepts are being described in new words, catch phrases, or sound bytes that pretend to reinvent original thought. In Coming To Terms With Acting we have not only the meanings of classic terms and concepts, but a simple and useful account of both the birth and evolution of this vocabulary.

Here in one small volume, the actor, director, playwright, or interested reader has access to a simple, lucid discussion of words and concepts that are still being thrashed about whenever theatre people gather. The short, concise definitions give an immediate understanding of each term and the detailed explanations provide a thorough understanding plus helpful instructions for performing each exercise.

There is an optimism in this book that is vital to any learning situation. Whenever we are in the position of not knowing something or not knowing what to do next, fear can set in. Here we have a practical key to understanding and unlocking artistic expression. To my knowledge, there is no other book like this on the market. Whether you are a theatre professional, or someone who is aspiring to theatre, this book not only clears up the confusion associated with the myriad concepts and their labels, it gives a clear understanding of what the creative process really is, and should be.

Frank Corsaro
Artistic Director
The Actors Studio

Preface

There is a part of our intellect that contains the answers to most of the questions our minds create. When we witness something new, we often sense a familiarity with it. "Yes, that makes sense," we might say. We are continually faced with new and original creations that amaze and delight us. At the same time there is often a deep understanding of the truth inherent in those creations. All things are possible within the laws of physics. The mind asks and the human spirit answers.

We are constantly searching for new ways, better ways, and easier ways to solve problems, take action, and increase the quality of our lives.

It is said that there is nothing new or original under the sun. All the elements have been here for millennia. How we assemble these old elements is what's new. There are infinite opportunities available to all of us. But with the new as with the old, there is always the familiar. Whether we recognize it or not, on a conscious level, we seek the familiar. We crave happiness, comfort, and security. All these are familiar. When you do something or when you create something, your efforts are received as something brand new, yet strangely familiar. Create means it never existed before. Your creation has the potential to unite us.

A century ago Constantin Stanislavski sought to make the performances he saw in the theatre look similar to what he observed in nature. He wanted to find a way to teach actors to create truth on the stage. What Stanislavski witnessed in the theatre of his time was a kind of representational acting that never tapped into a level of truth with which we're familiar.

There were some actors who did seem to transcend acting conventionally. Perhaps they were affected by something personal in performance. Or they felt a certain chemistry with their fellow actors. Either way, there was some unknown catalyst that provided inspiration in their work. These actors, Duse, Salvini, Mrs. Siddons among them, touched a truthful chord in their audiences. They were stars of their time just as we have stars today. Three thousand years ago I imagine there were stars as well.

In the theatre of ancient Greece an actor named Polus played in Sophocles' *Electra*. He had to express Electra's loss of Orestes and carry an urn on stage containing Orestes' ashes. In real life Polus had recently lost his own son. According to the earliest theatrical records we have, Polus brought out an urn containing the real ashes of his son. Wearing Electra's costume, he mourned, grieved, and expressed his genuine pain as though it were Electra's. This was not stage acting. This was not an imitation of truth, this was real. Real emotion was elicited. True feeling was expressed. Perhaps the back of the actor's wrist pressed against his forehead as he pleaded with the Gods gazing skyward.

Perhaps also, an out-of-work actor watched and felt the performance with his own intensity. Now the only way to express grief theatrically and properly is with the wrist-forehead mannerism. Every actor of the time does it that way now, whether he 'feels' it or not. Soon the original actor who played this is forgotten, but not the 'grief gesture.' It remains to haunt actor and audience alike far into the future. It remains because no one asked a question. "What is truth? What is it on the stage?" There was no curiosity about what was real, only a general acceptance of the 'symbol' for truth. No one questioned 'token truth.' There was no wondering about theatrical reality or theatrical truth. There was only theatrical imitation.

But, you might say, imitation is familiar! It is. It is familiar on the gross level. It lacks a certain depth to be truly substantial. Depth is a perspective that comes from curiosity, from asking questions. Asking questions in an impulsive, systematic way actually has the effect of creating higher intelligence.

I once saw an animal psychologist administer an IQ test to several puppies. He bounced toys and jingled stimuli in front of the puppies. Those pups that investigated where the sounds and movements originated, as opposed to those who just ignored them, were judged to be smarter. When we question each other, it is partly an attempt to identify with others. We want to feel comfortable with the people around us. To that end we seek familiarity. Finding the familiar becomes finding our place among the people around us, our family.

The terms discussed in this book are here to reacquaint you with what you may already sense. They are for you to use in your exploration and creation, your artistic expression of the new, the original, the familiar.

Doug Moston

Acknowledgments

The writing of a book is never a solo endeavor. The idea for the book occurred to me in 1979 after teaching my first acting class. During that class we found that each actor had his own idea of what was meant by the terms action, objective, intention, affective memory, emotional recall, etc. I visited my local theatre book store a day later to buy a book that defined and discussed the acting terms and concepts I was teaching. I learned there was no such book. I kicked around the idea of writing this book for the next twelve years. I would like to thank the individuals who helped me along the way.

I would never have begun this project without the encouragement and support of my friend for over thirty years, Sandy Woolworth. During the thirteen years I've taught my private classes I came to rely heavily on my two assistants. Julianne Ramaker took volumes of notes in class over the years that provided me with valuable references. Elizabeth Teal also took copious notes and, along with Julianne, helped me focus and clarify new thoughts and ideas into new strategies and exercises.

I am indebted to Stuart and Anne Vaughan, for their suggestions, support and inspiration. I am also grateful to my friend and colleague Patrick Tucker for his help and guidance on many sections of the book particularly the Shakespeare and verse technique sections.

I owe a special debt of thanks to Ralph Pine, Editor in Chief of Drama Book Publishers, whose advice and council proved invaluable. Barbara Haas, my editor, gave me excellent criticism and encouragement and to Judith Durant for her help and support. Without the continuous help, support, and cajoling of my wife Diana Moston, I don't think I would ever have finished this book.

I was also aided by the many ideas I gleaned from Edward Simon, PhD., Joann Galst, PhD., and Irving Weisberg, PhD.

Lastly I thank all of my students for the many lessons I have learned from them.

Introduction

This book is about defining the terminology used to teach and direct actors. It grew from a need to unify the jargon used by acting teachers, coaches, and directors and to help eliminate the confusion so often encountered by new and experienced actors, both in classes and in productions.

New actors are descending on the major markets of New York, Los Angeles, Chicago, and Florida every day, looking for workshops and classes. They are seeking acting teachers, coaches, classes, and any opportunity to learn and work at their craft.

There are many actors studying with countless numbers of teachers, all of whom teach differently. All teachers want to teach you to produce truthful, believable performances. With so many teachers and so many different approaches, the lack of a unified terminology often creates confusion. Confusion is one of the main obstacles in the way of forward movement. If you don't *understand* what to do, you *can't* do it. There are well-intentioned directors and teachers who make up their own terms. Often these terms are the product of a particular moment during a class or rehearsal. The director or teacher will use these terms to further his concept of the play to get certain results. The actor, who is taught never to go for results, must then 'translate' the terms into his process. It is the actor's process that will lead to the director's intended results. There are also teachers who make up terms, putting students at a disadvantage. Rather than talking of the character's objective, they're apt to ask what the character's 'dream-quest' is. It has the effect of taking the student out of the context of the discussion and inhibiting learning until he understands what the hell a 'dream-quest' is. The danger in the above instances is that made-up terms make actors dependent on their teachers. It is independence that cultivates true creativity.

What follows is a discussion of the most prevalent acting terms as they are used in classes, workshops, and productions, by teachers, coaches, and directors. There may not be an all-encompassing definition for each term, but you will get an overview of how the term is used and applied in today's theatre.

Ways To Use this Book

Of course, you can look up any term independently from the others. However, in order to understand better some entries you may need to read some of the other entries. Words appearing in SMALL CAPS are cross-references.

If you're in a hurry, you need only read the *quick definition* immediately following the term. If you want to know more, continue to read the full entry. If you need further details, consult the bibliography for specific books on the subject of your interest.

Pronouns

Sometimes my thinking involved women more than men. At other times I characterized my subject as 'he'. The term actor is applied to both males and females. My personal physician happens to be female; I do not refer to her as a doctress.

"Define, define, well-educated infant."

Shakespeare
Love's Labour's Lost
1594-5

"Every definition is dangerous."

Erasmus
Adagio
c. 1500

Accents and Dialects
Habits or characteristics of speech that help identify the background of the character.

If you don't have an ear for accents or dialects either learn them with books and records, get a dialogue coach, or don't use the accent or the dialect.

Frequently actors who are good at accents and dialects use them immediately when they get a part. This sometimes has the effect of hiding behind the CHARACTER. The enjoyment of the actor's natural ability to speak like the character makes him feel that he is the character when he talks like him. The problem is that unless the basic HOMEWORK is done, he will never create the illusion of a full character.

If you do have an ear for accents, try this as a way of using them in your work. Don't do the accent while you say your lines. Not at first, anyway. Do use the accent or dialect whenever you are not saying your lines. In REHEARSAL, when you're just talking to the director or the other actors, use the accent. When you're at home with friends, try out your accent for awhile. When you're in a restaurant or coffee shop talking to the waiter, talk in the accent. In this way you will be doing what the character does. You will be conducting your life using a particular way of speaking. In rehearsal, by not using the accent, you will be finding personal CHOICES that the accent can otherwise block. You will be rehearsing your character without the insulation of the accent.

About a week before you open, start using your accent with your lines. Your accent or dialect will not get in the way of doing what you and your character want to do.

Finally, your accent or dialect isn't simply there to show your character's geographical origins. For acting purposes know that your accent is also there to denote class. There is more than geography to consider in a scene between a Harvard professor from Cambridge and a student from Brooklyn, a person who speaks high British and one who speaks cockney. When you approach accents and dialects in this way, you will have far more to which you can relate and respond.

Action (internal or emotional)
What you do to get what your character wants.

Action is the SOUL of acting! It is the single most important concept to understand and apply properly. 'Properly' meaning responsibly, economically, and artistically.

Acting is doing. The Greek word, drama, according to the Oxford English Dictionary, means action, to do, to perform, to act. The moment our minds wander away from a play or a performance is usually the moment the action halts and the narrative[1] kicks in. "Show, don't tell" is the playwright's maxim. The actor's maxim should be "Do, don't show." In other words, don't illustrate, narrate, INDICATE, or pretend. Really do it!

A well written play is a series of events containing actions. When an actor assumes a CHARACTER, she or he must choose an action, in order to *do* the part, not just *narrate* the part.

How do you know what to do and when to do it? What to do comes from your character's OBJECTIVE, that is, what you want from the other character(s). As for when to do it, the answer is *always*. You are never on stage or in front of a camera doing nothing. Even when the text says you're to do nothing, you're doing something. You pace, try to read or sleep; you crack your knuckles, bite your nails, or adjust your appearance, but you do something. The only time you do nothing is when your character is dead.

---

[1] Narrative means you're talking about doing instead of really doing. In some class exercises actors are asked to express what they're feeling at the moment they're feeling it. Often you will see actors feel something either wonderful or painful. When asked to express what is happening to them using a sound, they describe or narrate it instead. Rather than narrating or saying "It feels great!", make a vocal sound that expresses it. That adds up to doing it as opposed to narrating it.

To choose an action that propels the play forward and helps to create your character, you must know your objective.

The objective, again, is what the character wants. It's in the text. You need $1000 from your boyfriend to pay the rent or you'll be evicted. Your objective? Get that money! And what do you do to your boyfriend to get the money? You pursue an *action*! Whether you use charm or intimidation, sex appeal or a pleading rationalization, you will use an action. And if that action is personal, something that has real meaning to you, you will create real conflict. Not a bad thing to do if you're in a play.

While you may not have many CHOICES regarding your objective, you have all the choices in the world in selecting an action.

A quick segue to the REHEARSAL process: your rehearsal is your opportunity to explore many different choices of actions.

If you rely on just thinking about choices, you'll cheat yourself out of the process of acting. Do it! Play it out loud two, three, or more times. In fact, play it as frequently as you need to, to see and feel which choices work best. By eliminating what you know doesn't work, you'll be left with those choices you know positively do work. Your extra, added bonus will be a built-in commitment to the choice. That commitment will release your full power or, what lay people call, "stage presence."

Why do you need a personal choice? Better yet, how do you make a personal choice? By following your instincts and expressing your IMPULSES as they happen. Acting is intuitive, not intellectual.

And now back to our story. So, you need $1000. Your boyfriend is the only one you know who has it, but he is going to buy the camcorder he's been saving for.

What you feel when you look at him and deal with him becomes the impulse for your choice of action. You might feel an impulse to flirt or seduce him. Or, depending on the PRIOR CIRCUMSTANCES and GIVEN CIRCUMSTANCES, or even your feelings about the actor playing your boyfriend, you could scold or embarrass him. Whatever you feel at that moment, you will *do* something to him. Your action will be SPECIFIC and actable.

It will be an action that can be physically accomplished. If it can be physicalized it will be specific.

3

Your action will always be a verb. If your action is: I'm going to make him feel like a small child in the principal's office. Ask yourself, *How do I do that?* You do it by breaking it down into very simple, specific, actable actions. To condescend, to intimidate, to threaten, etc.

Now you're pursuing your action with one hundred percent commitment and conviction and... lo and behold the boyfriend says, "But I'm not buying a camcorder. My grandma needs the money for an operation so she'll be able to walk again!" Curses! All you have to do is be willing to let your action go out the window in favor of what is happening now. If what he says affects you, then that stimulus will create in you a new response (IMPULSE). Trust it. Express it!

There are acting books that list pages of verbs as choices of action, as if you were making a selection from a restaurant menu. However, your choice of action must not only be a choice that involves you personally, it must also be a choice that expresses the INTENTIONS of the character as written by the playwright. If your choice leads you to tell your personal story at the expense of the playwright, rethink your choice. When you EXPLORE enough choices you'll know which one works best.

Incidentally, try not to deal with absolutes of right and wrong as far as actions go. It's more useful to deal with what's effective and what's not effective. If the action doesn't work, terrific! You've learned something that will get you closer to the action that does work. If you really explore a variety of actions, you will see that actions really do speak louder than words.

EXERCISE

What is your ACTION right now?

1. To read a book.
2. To seek a solution.
3. To plan an approach to your own work.
4. To improve your art.
5. None of the above.

Action (command in film)
This is the famous word that a movie director will say to cue you to act.

Wait a second! I mean wait a second or two after the director says "action!" It is often very useful in the editing room to have some footage of real behavior from the time the cameraman says "speed", indicating that the film is up to its proper speed, and the director says "action." The same is true after a director yells "cut!" Hold and stay in character for a few seconds. Sometimes your best reaction shots come from the moments when you're not acting, just before "action" and just after "cut".

Action (command in television)

By the way, in television you don't hear the command "action." Instead the director, from the control room, says through the mic to the stage manager, "In five...four...three...two..." the stage manager then repeats this and waives his arm broadly in place of "one." That's when you begin acting.

Activities
Activities are the physical things you do on stage. See also STAGE BUSINESS; TASKS.

A sustained piece of physical business on stage is an activity. In the Meisner[1] training this is often called having an 'independent physical activity'.

Some examples of activities are peeling an orange while you're carrying on with your dialogue, sorting your mail, washing dishes, putting away laundry, etc.

Whatever activity you choose must be important to you. And, most important, it must be difficult to do. It might even be impossible to do. I saw an actor do a MONO-

---

[1] Sanford Meisner was an original member of The Group Theatre in the 1930s. He has trained many stars in New York at The Neighborhood Playhouse, where he has headed the acting department for over forty years. Sanford Meisner invented the *Word Repetition Game*, which remains at the core of the Meisner Technique.

LOGUE from Gogol's *The Gambler*. In it he was boasting of his ability to cheat at cards. As he spoke, he readied himself for the next game. He carefully opened a sealed deck of cards from the bottom with a razor blade, and removed the aces. He hid them in his sock and resealed the pack with glue. It was all meticulously done while delivering the monologue. It was important and difficult. From doing the activity and dealing with the OBSTACLE, an emotion resulted. The activity you choose, scripted or not, can tell us more about your CHARACTER, your RELATIONSHIP, and your emotional state.

Adding an activity can be just the right CHOICE to make a scene work by physically clarifying the character's INTENTIONS and your ACTIONS.

Adjustments
Changes in the directions (actions) you are given, or the choices you've made.

An adjustment today is the way a director or a teacher changes or influences your CHOICES, or what it is that you are doing. During Vakhtangov's[1] time, an adjustment would let the actor incorporate directorial changes while still in CHARACTER and still in the situation.

It could be a minor adjustment, such as "Don't face your partner until he says 'Hold me!'" Or something major, like "Instead of charming her when you enter, ignore her."

Directors will make adjustments either because what you're doing isn't working or because what you've just found in rehearsal gave the director a better idea.

When a director gives you an adjustment in an audition situation, it is one of the best signs in your favor. It generally means he sees something in you and is testing your flexibility, or possibly matching you with the rest of his prospective cast. In either case, it is an extra opportunity for you to show more of yourself, your work, and your talent.

---

[1] Evgeny Vakhtangov was a student of Stanislavski at the Moscow Art Theatre (First Studio). Vakhtangov adapted and reformulated many of Stanislavski's concepts. He headed the Third Studio of the Moscow Art Theatre in 1920, which became the Vakhtangov Theatre. He was a major influence on Lee Strasberg and became one of Russia's greatest teachers and directors. He died in 1922.

Affective Memory
Exploring, or creating a past event from your life for use in a scene or character. Also called emotional memory or emotional recall.

Lee Strasberg[1], after his initial discovery of affective memory, divided affective memory into two categories. SENSE MEMORY and EMOTIONAL MEMORY. Today, however, the terms affective memory, emotional memory and EMOTIONAL RECALL are mostly used interchangeably. There are certain distinctions that some METHOD practitioners make that will be discussed under the specific term.

Affective memory is one of those famous, controversial method exercises. It is based in sense memory. By going back into your past and questioning all the SENSORY elements of a specific event, you can re-experience that event and discover many nuances of original behavior. These are expressed in the present. It is important to understand this point.

On the other side of the argument was Stella Adler's[2] assertion that the "undue emphasis on 'affective memory' warped the actor." Ms. Adler visited STANISLAVSKI in Paris because she felt that parts of the system frustrated her. Stanislavski replied that if it gets in your way, don't use it. But, he added, perhaps you don't understand it. She then spent five weeks in Paris with Stanislavski coaching her privately in a scene from *The Gentle Woman*. That was the play in which Strasberg directed her before she left for Paris. Stanislavski taught her that, "The source of acting is imagination and the key to its problems is truth, truth in the circumstances of the play."

Much of the controversy surrounding affective memory today has to do with the psycho-exploitational aspects of the way the exercise has been done in different acting classes.

Actors should always make the CHOICES as to which events they want to explore. If they make the choices, it indicates that they are ready to deal with them. Some teachers, having inside knowledge about a student's

---

[1] *A Dream of Passion*, Boston: Little, Brown & Co., 1987
[2] Stella Adler, *The Technique of Acting*, New York: Bantam Books, 1988

past, may suggest an event the actor may find psychologically difficult.

Another trap with affective memory is the motive for doing the exercise. Many actors are trying to find an emotion or feeling. They are ignoring their process and going directly to the perceived result. In effect, they learn to push a button to make themselves cry, get angry, or whatever. Using the exercise to find a SPECIFIC emotion is not the same as using it to explore behavior.

In order to try an affective memory exercise yourself, choose an event that has an emotional significance to you. It should be at least five years in the past. You need some distance in order to be able to use it and not have it use you.

Sit in a straight chair with no arms and find a position in which you could fall asleep. Close your eyes, RELAX and take a few deep breaths. In your mind, begin going back in time to just before the event. Now start asking questions that deal with the sensory elements of the event. Is it daytime or night? What is it that you hear? Voices? Whose? What are they saying? What do you see in front of you? Are you indoors or outside? Do you smell anything? What specifically are you wearing?

It is best to work this exercise with a responsible teacher or director who is experienced in guiding the exercise. You should also have an understanding of why you're doing it. Is there an element missing in your CHARACTER, or your scene? Are you representing a cliché emotion instead of expressing your uniqueness? Is it for INSTRUMENT or CRAFT development in class? Whatever your results are, you should be able to apply them to your work.

Animal Exercises
Using the essence of a specific animal to physicalize a character.

"He's as sly as a fox", "She's so catty", "He's like a bull in a china shop", "He's a teddy bear". These clichés illustrate the essence of 'animal' work.

There are times when an actor gets stuck on his approach to creating a role. The CHARACTER element he's searching for seems elusive, to say the least. Often, if he can physicalize the character, other elements begin to fall into place.

When you work on an animal exercise you are not trying to imitate the animal. Although the process begins with imitating the animal, it quickly moves into a discovery of the animal's essence. By starting to imitate the sluggishness of an elephant you trigger your own sluggishness. When you explore the quickness of a cat you find your own quickness. If the essence of a particular animal captures the essence of your character and the 'quality' you're striving for is not naturally in you (by the way, you can't play a quality, you can play an 'action'), animal work might be just the ticket.

Once, while performing several characters in a children's show, a friend was stuck on how to create the role of the baron, an old, grouchy, Jewish gentleman who was hard of hearing. The clichés were all too predictable. That Sunday, he was walking near the pond in Central Park watching the ducks and admiring how cute they looked. He said he realized that instead of just watching the ducks, perhaps he should OBSERVE them as well. He noticed one particular duck pecking at the other ducks to get at their food. As he looked at the duck's face and eyes, he could see that this duck wasn't cute at all. This duck's face was mean. He made darting, quick movements of his head in response to the other ducks and his quacks expressed annoyance.

My friend went home and created the duck's face on his own face. He pursed his lips slightly to get the sense of a duck's bill. He used his head and eyes in unison to scan for food, and he extended the essence through his spine to walk, or waddle, and use his wings (arms) to flap away any disturbances. When he played the barron, he wore age make-up, a beard, and a bathrobe. His first lines were, "What? What's that you say?" This in response to the maid asking if he wanted some tea. When I finally saw the performance, I could have sworn that the 'what' sounded just like a 'quack'.

There are, of course, some famous examples of animal work. Marlon Brando used an ape to create the physicality of Stanley Kowalski in *A Streetcar Named Desire*. Lee J. Cobb used an elephant to establish the lumbering quality of Willy Loman carrying valises his whole life in *Death of a Salesman*.

There was an actor in class with whom, for many reasons, people were not lining up to work. After working on a specific puppy for several weeks he was able to

9

loosen up and get to a part of himself that was always missing from his work. When he became the puppy, it amazed us to see how many students would call him over to pet him and hold him. Using an animal exercise, he found a quality within him that attracted people and deepened his character.

Working on an animal exercise begins with detailed observation of a SPECIFIC animal. It shouldn't be a dog or a monkey. It should be a particular dog or monkey that you can study every day. If you don't have a pet, go to the park or the zoo. You can even use a video tape of an animal.

Observe the animal's breathing and breathe that way. Find the physical center of the animal. In a cat it's the spine. In a cow it's the torso, etc. Sit, stand, and move in the way the animal does. Handle OBJECTS in the same way. If a monkey picks up a glass, he will wrap his fingers and thumb together around the glass. Examine the OBSTACLES to how the animal moves and what he wants to do.

After you get the physical sense of the animal, work for the animal's sound. If you're working on a cat, avoid the high pitched "meow" that you hear the actual animal make. The animal is releasing it's own natural sound. You must release your own natural sound, which will of necessity, be deeper in accordance with your size. The "meow" will be your own natural voice.

One of the great benefits of animal work is the lack of ego that comes from being the animal. I've seen actors who are inhibited in scenes, become centered doing animal work. The animal's essence unlocks the key to the actor's and the character's essence.

Anticipation
Basing your choices on the fact that you know what happens next.

Anticipation is what happens when the actor knows his CHARACTER's future. As an actor, you get to read the end of the play. You know what your co-star will say and do in response to you. In short, you always know what will happen next. And if your INVOLVEMENT is in the future, it's hard to make an audience believe that your character is in the present.

10

Stanislavski said that the actor's greatest problem was 'anticipation'. That was true in the early 1900s. Today, however, the actors greatest problem is getting work! Sounds funny, but it's true. Back then, directors and actors could afford to spend six months to a year to work on one role. Today, everything is instant. We watch political figures in the news make instant assessments and appraisals of complex situations because there is a television camera trained on them. They are concerned with image. They are under pressure to have immediate answers. They are the authors of the fifteen-second sound bytes. They are focused on the future in order to anticipate correctly what to do next.

Most acting techniques are designed to keep your focus in the present. If you know your CHARACTER must cry at the end of the scene, you may be tempted to find a way to force your emotions, to make yourself cry. Your attention is in the future. The character, on the other hand, is dealing with the present situation and conditions. As an actor, you need to do the same.

Stanislavski told a story about one of his own performances in Gorky's *The Lower Depths*. He said that he had so much on his mind regarding day-to-day, real life problems in addition to acting problems in the play, that he became totally absorbed and stopped worrying about the play, his acting problems and his personal problems. Stanislavski:

> I did not even act that evening, but just carried out the *tasks* of my part logically and consistently in words and ACTION. Logic and consistency led me along the right road, and the part acted itself and I never noticed its weak points. As a result my performance became of great importance to the play, though I never even thought of it.

EXERCISE

When about to enter a dark room, do you...

1. Turn on the lights?
2. Try to find the light switch?
3. Light a match?
4. Not go in the room?

Arena Stage
A stage where the audience is seated around three sides.

Arena is an old Latin word for the sand that was used to absorb the blood of the Gladiators and the Christians fighting lions in Roman times—cheerful thought.

An arena stage is technically a stage in the center of the auditorium or THEATRE IN THE ROUND.

Today, an arena stage is one that has an audience on three sides. If you are playing UPSTAGE in an arena stage, more of the audience will see you. If you are playing DOWNSTAGE you will cut out about two thirds of the house.

As-If (Magic If)
Programming yourself to behave 'as if'" a certain condition existed. Also referred to as the 'creative if' and the 'magic if.'

> If thou, perforce, acquir'd the right mannor,
> Then from a Tablet, could one strut some stuff
> Upon the stage. Thus, playing tough, not puff.

In other words, I can't write a book *as* Shakespeare because I'm *not* Shakespeare, but I can write 'as if' I were Shakespeare.

Harold Clurman, in his book *On Directing,*[1] wrote that a performance will be different if an actor enters the stage as if he were entering a cathedral or if he behaves in a room, as if a bomb were to explode. The power of the 'as if', or 'magic if', is great.

Try talking to a friend as if he had just inherited several million dollars or as if he had a terminal disease. Does your behavior change? Handle the three-dollar prop bowl as if it was a twelfth-century Chinese antique. Once after watching an actor do a MONOLOGUE and seeing he was filled with tension while trying to play a really cool, relaxed CHARACTER, the director simply asked him to play it as if he were relaxed and really cool. He did it and it worked.

The wonderful thing about the 'as if' concept is that it will stimulate the IMAGINATION to new heights. If you're

---

1 London: Collier Macmillan Publishers, 1972

stuck, you might begin your CHOICES with any 'as if' at all. See what happens. When you fully experience the value of the 'as if' in your work, you'll quickly understand why it's also called the 'magic if.'

Aside
When the character breaks away from the situation to talk to the audience without being heard by the other characters.

How many times have we seen an actor leave one or more actors on stage and turn to us to tell us what's really going on? It's often my favorite time in a play, because I'm invited to participate instead of just being a spectator. It also reinforces the TRUTH of the theatrical metaphor. It acknowledges the fact that there really is an audience taking part in the play.

Some questions to ask when dealing with asides should be: What is the RELATIONSHIP between my CHARACTER and the people (audience) I'm talking to? Are they simply audience members? Are they courtesans, board members, family members, or other group? A SPECIFIC CHOICE must be made.

Audition
A talent test. The procedure of observing the work of actors to determine who is best suited to play a role.

An audition is the best way there is of finding out who gets to play the part. Even when a director knows a particular actor's work, she or he may still not be certain of how the actor will handle the CHARACTER or match up with the rest of the cast or the director's concept.

Actors are generally of two minds about auditions. They will break their necks to get an audition for a coveted role. As soon as they get it, they dread it. Auditions are scary but not for everyone. There are some actors who see auditioning in a healthy perspective. They have developed audition skills and look forward to using them. They view an audition as a chance to show their work and network their careers. Their outlook is positive and creative. It is not based on fear. Fear is the enemy of creativity.

Guess who else isn't wild about auditions—directors. Directors can sometimes be just as uncomfortable as you are. Most directors would rather work with actors they know. Because so much of directing is casting, there's a lot of pressure on the director to find the 'perfect' cast. Directors don't enjoy rejecting people. They don't want to make you feel nervous and uncomfortable. Believe it or not, every director wants you to get the part. The moment you walk through the door, the director's hoping you will be the one.

So we have two groups of people, both sometimes wishing they could be doing something else, thrust together to determine whether there will be a creative, artistic, working relationship resulting from the audition process.

The actors are outside the audition room or studio, or in the wings of the theatre waiting. They are sitting talking a mile a minute to their friends or they're quiet and introspective. They're studying the material, hoping, wondering, praying, and desperately trying to figure out how to exterminate the butterflies that laid siege to their stomachs. Now it's your turn. You go into the audition room or on to the stage. You're confronted with the ubiquitous table. You on one side and 'them' on the other. Who are on the other side of the table and what the hell are they looking for?

On the director's side of the table

...sits the director surrounded by people. The production stage manager (has a say in casting) might be there, the producer (has a say in casting), a casting director, some assistants, the musical director, the choreographer, lyricist, and the playwright (who has a very definite say in casting). Of course it might be only the director. It might also be all of the above. They all want the audition to go smoothly, meaning that if the show has a cast of four, the first four actors will be perfect. Then they can all go home. Of course, it never happens that way.

They watch you enter. They size you up. How do you walk? Do you make eye contact? Are you being yourself? Are you *prepared* with your picture and résumé in hand, or do you say, "Wait a minute!"—and take up valuable time while you hunt through your bag?

You approach the director and say, "Hello". Don't expect to be introduced. Can you imagine going through fifty introductions a day? The director may take a moment to see if you look like your picture and look over your resumé. If you don't look like the person in the picture and they've called you in because of your picture, you've just wasted everyone's time. But that isn't *your* problem. Your picture looks exactly like you, but on your best day. The director may ask about your résumé. He may get you to talk about one of your credits. He may ask where you've studied. He and the others behind the table want you to have read the audition instructions that were in the paper or that were given to you by your agent. They are hoping you will not come in and say, "Tell me about what you're doing."

He will then ask what you will do for your audition, provided it isn't a COLD READING from the play, or a prepared scene. If it's a MONOLOGUE, he's hoping you will be thoroughly prepared and that you won't ask him if you can take a minute to PREPARE. He's hoping you won't spend time telling him what happened in the play just before your speech. He doesn't care. He wants you to come in, do the monologue and leave, unless you're asked to stay, either to talk more or because the director wants to give you an ADJUSTMENT. He may even ask you to read for a different part. One that you don't see yourself playing. You, of course, will not tell him that.

The director is hoping you will have different levels of emotion and behavior in your work. The director is hoping you will make CHOICES that will tell the story of the play, if you are reading from the play. But if your choices are absolutely wrong the director won't care. As

15

ALLEGHENY COLLEGE LIBRARY

long as you make big choices and commit to them fully, the director can give you other, 'more correct' choices. When you're finished he will say, "Thank you," and it means he wants you to leave and not ask how you did. There isn't enough time to have that discussion.

They hope that when you leave the audition room, you will walk confidently out the door and not into an adjacent wall. They hope that your hand finds the door knob right away and that you don't trip and hurt yourself.

On your side of the table

You walk in prepared with your picture and résumé in one hand, your bag and coat in the other. You are dressed appropriately for the part. That is, if your playing a banker, you wear a suit. For a hooker, you wear something sexy, but not the actual costume of a hooker. Wear something that will allow the director to visualize you in the part.

You greet your auditors and smile. You will not apologize for your résumé. Whatever you've done is whatever you've done. People become actors at all different ages, therefore age is not a factor in determining experience in the theatre. You can express your creativity on your résumé. One picture and résumé I'll never forget was from an actor in his thirties. On the back of his picture was a résumé printed on pink paper. It had his name and service number. Diagonally across the page was printed one large word, Virgin. He got called.

You will not apologize for anything unless you do something blatantly terrible, like knock over the table. Actors are the most creative people in the world when it comes to finding ways of apologizing for just about anything, including who they are. Cut it out! You will not worry about what they're looking for. You will not be influenced by other actors' stories about who they are and what they want. You don't know, you won't know, and often they don't know either.

You either tell them the name of your monologue or you set about reading your SIDES immediately. If you're doing a prepared monologue, you should do one that best 'sells' who you are. One that is professionally responsible, meaning that if you're nineteen you're not going in there to play Blanche DuBois. If you're reading with the stage manager, you will make choices that reflect that you're talking to the character even though the stage manager reads 'flat', with no emotion. You will not get mad at the stage manager. You will use your script if it's a reading. You will not try to memorize the part. Professionals know that to turn in a performance without REHEARSAL is crazy. They're asking you to read. So read!

When you leave, you thank the director. You will then forget the audition. After all, you have three more auditions today. You cannot allow yourself to be thrown by a bad audition no matter whose fault it was.

If there is a way for you to sit on the other side of the table, do it. Maybe you can volunteer at a theatre company and assist with an audition. Perhaps you know a producer or a director who will let you watch. The best way to learn about auditions is to sit on the director's side of the table. You'll get to see exactly what to do. And what not to.

When you have an audition try to prepare everything and anything you can. If there is an ACCENT or DIALECT involved, work on it. If there are certain MANNERISMS called for, study them. If you wake up feeling lousy, do something to change your mood for your audition.

When you arrive at the audition site keep your focus. Don't dissipate your ENERGY by talking nervously with the other actors, even your friends. If you see a friend who needs to talk to you, tell him politely that you are preparing, or trying to learn a monologue for your class tonight and ask him out for coffee after the audition.

Learn to see auditions as opportunities to demonstrate your art. Make them challenging, fun, and often.

Beats

One unit of text denoting the beginning and end of an action. Or simply, a moment, as in "wait two beats and continue".

Many teachers and directors break text down into BEATS, or units of ACTIONS, OBJECTIVES, or INTENTIONS. Unfortunately the terms actions, objectives, and intentions are often used interchangeably.

Stanislavski counseled actors to divide the role into units so they will always have simple, actable CHOICES to play that are connected to one overall objective, which Stanislavski called the SUPER-OBJECTIVE. The marking of beats or units along the way to the super objective, the path itself, he called the channel.

In Stanislavski's example, the main objective might be to go home. The first beat is to go downstairs, the second to stop and look in the window of a book store, the third to open the door, the fourth to get undressed, and so on. By following the 'channel' you insure that the beats you play will keep you on the path to your main objective.

"Always remember," Stanislavski cautions, "that the division is temporary. The part and the play must not remain in fragments.... During the actual creation they fuse into large units."[1]

Many actors break a play down and proceed with actions and objectives that are personal, but have little

---

1 *An Actor Prepares* (New York: Theatre Arts Books, 1936).

or nothing to do with the CHARACTER or the play. Not only does the actor become confused, the audience does too. That is why the beats or units must follow a logical channel.

If your objective is to propose marriage to your lover, your first beat might be to impress, then to charm, then to tease, then possibly to seduce. All of these could be EXPLORED in REHEARSAL. But stick to the channel and allow the beats to join together eventually.

In Mrs. Hapgood's[2] translation of Stanislavski, there are claims that Stanislavski didn't really talk about beats at all, but that he was saying 'bit' and that his Russian accent made it sound like beat, "We will see the next *bit*." Regardless, the concept of units (or beats if you wish), is not only spelled out clearly in the literature but it is of inestimable value to the actor today.

Blocking
The physical arrangement of the actors' movements on stage.

Directors have many approaches to blocking, depending on the play's being presented. Some directors let actors arrive at there own blocking through rehearsal and then make minor ADJUSTMENTS so there are no 'traffic jams.' Of course, some plays demand to be pre-blocked.

When a director pre-blocks a play, he will generally use a model of the set with cut-out characters or sometimes a chess board with chess pieces for the actors. He will then work out optimum patterns of movement, where and how best to direct the 'third eye' of the audience and pay close attention to 'sightlines'[1], depending on the layout of the theatre itself.

Blocking should serve to tell the story physically. If a character is emotionally caught between two other

---

[2] Elizabeth Reynolds Hapgood translated much of Stanislavski's work into English including his three main books *An Actor Prepares*, *Building a Character*, and *Creating a Role*, all published by Theatre Arts Books, 1936, 1949, and 1961 respectively.

---

[1] Literally the lines of sight so that all of the audience can see all of the actors and the action being presented on the stage. Directors often ask actors to move up or downstage for reasons of sightlines alone. In rehearsal directors will seat themselves in different seats at different times around the theatre in order to check for sightlines.

characters, his parents for example, begin by blocking the actor between Mom and Dad.

In many style pieces, much attention is paid to 'picturization,' literally a way of creating a picture or sometimes a tableau that tells the play's story. Directors often study great paintings for ideas in staging and blocking a scene.

As we are accustomed, in western civilization, to reading from left to right, we are most comfortable seeing from left to right as well. This principle is very useful in blocking a scene. If the good guy enters from STAGE RIGHT, and crosses left, our eyes will easily follow him. Contrast that with the villain entering from STAGE LEFT where our eyes work against what we're used to, enhancing the feeling we want from the villain. In light of the above, one of the most powerful points on the stage is stage left or left of center stage. It is where our eye wants to go.

Costumes will also influence blocking. If a costume is particularly elaborate, such as you might find in a Shakespearean production, you will want the character facing out much of the time. The second most powerful position on stage is with one's back to the audience. Profile is the weakest.

Actors who are trained to EXPLORE a role carefully are often uncomfortable when asked by the director to begin the process with blocking. They would prefer instead to let the blocking evolve from their work. Other classically trained actors are thrown by a director who blocks the play towards the end of the REHEARSAL process. They want to know where they're going from the start. Since there are directors who work both ways depending on the play, it's a good idea for actors to adopt a flexible approach. When you condition yourself to view a problem as a challenge, your talent and creativity can 'kick in' and the solution will often be something of which you can be proud.

Breakthrough
The point at which you either overcome an obstacle and/or reach a new emotional level previously unattainable.

You've heard your teacher say something over and over. Finally it clicks. Your performance is now total. You can finally say, "I own it". *ZAPP!* You've had a breakthrough.

Twenty years ago on the New York acting scene people talked about breakthroughs more than they seem to today. When an actor cried for the first time in an exercise or a scene we referred to it as his emotional breakthrough. If an actress fully expressed her rage for the first time publicly, that was her emotional breakthrough.

Breakthroughs became so desirable that people would talk about actors in terms of whether or not they had had a breakthrough. If they hadn't yet, then they weren't as highly respected as those who had.

Consequently, if you hadn't experienced a breakthrough, you needed one. You worked for one. You weren't really an actor without one. Ouch!

Breakthroughs are like ideas, you can't make them happen. They are immune to force. Breakthroughs are results, byproducts of the work, of trusting your process.

When you become aware that you are unintentionally withholding who you are and not expressing everything that is going on within you, you've taken the first step. You have defined the problem in your conscious mind and set for yourself a goal. Having set the goal, your next order of business is to leave yourself alone. You must trust that you have 'programmed' your creativity to find a solution to overcoming the OBSTACLE. When you're relaxed and doing your job properly, when you're in the MOMENT, that's when a breakthrough will likely occur.

Callback
A request to repeat your audition.

If you feel your AUDITION went well. And 'they' feel your audition went well, you will get a callback. This means you're getting closer to getting the job.

Directors have callbacks to narrow down their choices of who will play the part. There may be one or several callbacks depending on the nature of the project being cast. The callback gives them another look at you and your work. They will often match you up with the rest of their prospective cast in the callback. This may be your chance to read with the star of the show. If your first audition was a prepared MONOLOGUE, you may be asked to read from the script. If you originally read from the script, you may be called back to read a different scene, even a different part.

When you get a callback, try to do the same, exact thing you did in the original audition. That is why you're being called back. Resist the temptation to 'make it better'. Making it better means you're changing it. Be careful.

Wear the same clothes you wore in your first audition. Frequently directors remember and refer to an actor based on what he or she wore to the audition. "Callback the guy with the bow tie, the guy wearing yellow suspenders, and the girl in the silver lamé dress" is not an uncommon request from a director to a stage manager. We called back an actress once who auditioned wearing turquoise pants. When she arrived at the callback, five days later, not only did she wear the same pants, we noticed her résumé was printed on turquoise paper. Anything and everything can help.

Understand this. When you get a callback, whether you get the part or not, it means they're interested in you. They like you. If you get the part, terrific. If you don't, it isn't you. It has nothing to do with your talent. Once you are called back, your work has a stamp of approval. The reason you may not get the job is usually technical. You're too tall or too short. Your hair is the wrong color, etc.

If you're getting a lot of callbacks for the same project, don't get discouraged. They're trying to work out a problem that has nothing to do with you. Be patient. Be as nice as you can be. Even if it's your twentieth call for the same project. It happens. Stay cool.

Character
The person whom you are playing.

"Who creates the character?" You might be surprised how many actors answer, "The actor does." It is, of course, the playwright who creates the character, the actor who creates the role.

22

Having said that, it is amazing how many actors still use themselves (a good thing to do) at the expense of creating the character that the author wrote (not so good). Sometimes you'll be lucky and be cast precisely because of who you are (TYPE casting). But this mostly happens in film and television. Part of the fun of acting is creating different roles, different people, and people different from us.

Think of character attributes as responses to stimuli. First, investigate each stimulus. If the character were raised in the South, she might speak more slowly, not to mention in a southern accent. If, however, she were raised in a family of fast talkers, then perhaps in order to survive and fit in, she is a fast talker too. How does she handle hot weather? Does she limp, stutter, have a characteristic laugh? All these questions and more benefit from EXPLORATION. Many of the answers are supplied by the author as GIVEN CIRCUMSTANCES.

A character may also have a belief system different from yours. You may be outgoing and gregarious, while the character might be shy and introverted. Creating the SPECIFIC stimuli that make you shy will lead to the right CHOICES for your character. Often playing a certain character will be a very freeing experience for the actor, as he or she now has permission to go OVER THE TOP with behavior that is usually risky.

An exercise you can try now or in class is to physicalize a character by consciously changing, adjusting, or slightly exaggerating a part of your own physicality. For instance, jut your chin out, just a little. Take a moment to experience the change. Does it elicit a feeling within you? A person different from you may start to emerge. Maybe it's someone you know. Now talk as this person and move around the room. Discover what MANNERISMS come into play in order for this character to express him or herself.

What do we mean when we speak of a character actor as opposed to a leading man? The leading man is a character too, isn't he? For that matter, we often speak of people who aren't actors at all as characters, meaning, that they behave in a manner that is different from us. We either like the difference or we don't. We're interested or we're not.

If we find only the outward characteristics of the character we are to play, we will wind up with a caricature at best; an outline, a sketch, or easily identified cartoon of a whole individual.

To create a *full* character we must find the SOUL of the character. We must know who he is in relation to ourselves and our partners. We must know what he stands for, what motivates him, what he needs and wants from others and for himself. We must know what he wants from life. We must then actively pursue these goals AS IF they were our own.

Your natural curiosity is the best material with which to build a character. If you're not feeling particularly curious today you might employ a 'character inventory.' Enjoy investigating the following questions. What time do you live in? Are you an American Indian fighting for your nation's territory in the early 1800s? Are you exploring new galaxies in a state of the art space vessel? What is your education? How well do you use words and articulate ideas? What are your religious beliefs? Do you believe in God? What clothes make you most comfortable, most uncomfortable? To what class do you belong? Do you speak with an ACCENT? If so, remember that an accent indicates not only geographical designation, but class differences as well. What do you do for a living? Are you the Sheriff of Dodge City, Nottingham, or are you the Prince of Denmark? Are you homeless, or are you in government? What are your character attributes? Are you often depressed, grumpy, or angry? Are you filled with ambition? Are you ruthless, or are you described as a pushover? Are you a quiet intellectual about to find the cure for the common cold? Or are you an extroverted entertainer creatively covering low self-esteem? All of these questions plus many more demand your creative attention.

When you answer these questions, approach speculation with caution. Are you making up the answers or are you getting them from the character's creator, the playwright. Remember, all you know about your character for dead certain is that he or she says the words that are on the page.

Choices
What you do or tell yourself in order to create the role.

When the actor playing the villain succeeds in affecting us because he played the scoundrel as charming, he is simply executing a CHOICE, to be charming instead of villainous. When you make a choice that has a personal meaning to you, your behavior will be more compelling to watch because you will be more committed, therefore more INVOLVED in your choice.

Positive choices are better than negative choices and big choices are better than small ones. Positive choices are choices that contribute to the action of the play, or the action of the character. To kill, for example, is not a negative choice, theatrically speaking, because it will enhance the drama. Or rather, we hope it will. On the other hand, to kill in life would obviously be a negative.

What is a negative choice for an actor? To wait. Boring! A negative choice is also the way in which you 'program' yourself. In other words, how you tell yourself what to think and what to do. In choosing something positive, the part becomes easier to play. For example, I'm going to intimidate him or I'm going to try to impress her. I can't play the negative, that is, to try *not* to impress, or to try *not* to intimidate. Just restate the choice to yourself. Rather than trying not to intimidate, make your ACTION to calm your partner. Instead of trying not to impress, you can choose to distance yourself from or even ignore your partner. The point is to think through any choice you're PREPARING and EXPLORE it in REHEARSAL.

One problem that new actors frequently encounter is what choices to make. The reason it's sometimes difficult is that actors don't give themselves things from which to choose, a 'choice menu' so to speak. Only by exploring different ways of playing a scene can you choose properly which way works best for you, the director, the playwright, and most importantly, the audience.

Guernica is not only the name of a town in Spain that was ravaged by the revolution, it is also the name of one of Picasso's greatest paintings. The painting is large, both in size, power, and artistic ingenuity. It depicts the suffering of the Guernican people at the hands of the fascists and the inhumanity of war. For as long as I can remember, it hung in New York at the Museum of Modern Art. Picasso did not want it in Spain until fascism was renounced there. The painting is in black and white. This huge canvas with life-sized people makes an impact on your head and heart in black and white. But before it was returned to Spain, after the death of dictator Francisco

Franco, it made it's last appearance in New York as part of a special Picasso Show chronicling the artists life work. Accompanying the Guernica were Picasso's studies for it. They were in color! If Picasso did all these studies in brilliant colors, why then did he choose to create the final work in black and white?

In the 1930s public information came visually through the media of newspapers and newsreels, both of which were in black and white. As gifted a colorist as Picasso was, you can imagine the impact the image had when presented in black and white.

The element of choice is what makes you an artist. A good friend who is a wonderful actor said that when he is at an AUDITION, he finds the obvious choice and then goes right to the OPPOSITE. And that's only how he starts his process. An actor I know was playing in a serious drama that concludes with the death of his soul mate. Now personally, the actor hated the actress playing his lover. He was probably thrilled when, lying on her deathbed, she expired. Despite his real feelings about her, his performance was riveting. The audience was grief stricken along with his CHARACTER when he quietly broke down in reaction to her death. In the actor's real life his sister was suffering from a terminal disease. One night after the show I asked him what his choice was for the death scene. "Did you use your sister?" I remember vividly the way he answered. "No," he said, and he smiled, "when I looked down at her in that bed, I never saw my sister, I saw myself."

Many actors stop creating after they discover the obvious choice. "Oh, she's upset", they say, "I'll play upset". It isn't that simple. There are people who can read a page of music and know whether or not they like the melody. Most of us have to hear it played or sung. Good plays are similarly scored. Try beginning your process by saying the words out loud. You will have the beginnings of a 'choice menu' just by hearing the words aloud as opposed to merely reading them.

Another way of applying the term choice comes from my British colleagues. Here, we ask our character to *choose* to do or say a certain thing. In Shakespeare, for example, when the character ends her speech in a rhyming couplet, "A drum, a drum, Macbeth doth come," don't be tempted to smooth it out to make us think that's the way you really talk. Instead, ask your character to choose to rhyme the two lines because your character *wants* to. The playwright, after all, has chosen those words for the character to say, in order to *create* the character.

Cliché
A mannerism or approach to a role that has been done before, many times.

When the villain comes on and twists his mustache to let you know who he is, he is acting a cliché. When the actor playing Lady Macbeth chooses to tyrannize those around her, she too is playing a stage cliché.

A cliché is the avoidance of creativity. A theatrical cliché is similar to a verbal cliché in that it serves to limit the precision of communication. When the cliché was born, it wasn't a cliché, it was original. For it to endure as a cliché, it had to be continuously repeated. Something was said or done that served to express an idea, a thought, a particular meaning in an accurate and original way. This became so admired and approved, that to do something different was to do something less than admirable and incur the risk of disapproval.

There is an argument that says, if a cliché is repeated so often it must be an excellent way of expressing whatever the idea is. Yes. And no! Yes, it will serve the purpose of communication. No, it will not be creative. It will not be ORGANIC, that is originating in the MOMENT from within the artist who is responding to stimuli right then and there.

Cold Reading
Reading aloud, from the script, with no rehearsal.

In a proper cold reading the actor will be given somewhere between five and thirty minutes to read over the part before either AUDITIONING or reading publicly. But he is performing in any case. That's the usual custom, but there are no set rules. There are those times when an actor will be asked to read without even casting an eye on the piece. "Here, read this," commands the director, and the actor will often comply happily. These are often called ice cold readings.

Cold readings mostly occur at auditions. Actors either love them or hate them depending on whether or not they are good at them.

Some actors are naturally good at cold readings. This is because there is no pressure to make so-called correct CHOICES. Since their is no REHEARSAL, there is no obligation to achieve any SPECIFIC moment that might have been found in a rehearsal. The actors are free to take risks, make big personal choices, and, if they don't tell the story of the play properly, the director can then give them more information or ADJUSTMENTS and allow the actors another go at it. "Also," as Alan Alda says, "cold readings have nothing to do with acting. You can be brilliant in a cold reading but there's no guarantee that you'll be able to repeat it."

On the other hand, many wonderful actors hate cold readings simply because they have never developed the skill necessary to do them well.

If you struggle with cold readings, buy yourself a children's book printed in large type. Practice reading from the book by using your finger to mark the words as you read. Read the thought, or sentence, then mark with your finger the beginning of the next small section, look up and simply convey the meaning of what you've just read to the listener. Then look back down to the page to see the next part of the story, mark it with your finger again, and repeat the process. It takes some practice but it works.

Some casting directors feel that, at times, an actor should gracefully avoid cold readings in audition situations. If you're not good at the technique, then try to get the script in advance and PREPARE. Most casting directors will accommodate you even if it's only to let you read the script in their waiting rooms.

EXERCISE

Select a magazine advertisement with a small amount of copy. Use a mirror and read the copy out loud, to yourself while looking up as often as you can.

Collusion

Inadvertently going along with your partner to the detriment of the scene and your work.

Collusion is not an official acting term. You won't find it in any of the books on theatre. Colluding with your partner means you agree to overlook less than adequate work on both your parts. It says you agree to substandard work. Because this phenomenon occurs subconsciously, you may not be aware of it when it's happening

Here's how collusion can affect the creative theatre situation. When actors, in rehearsal, simply don't believe another actor's behavior and they go along with it because they know what the fake behavior is supposed to be, they are engaging in collusion. What to do if it happens to you?

First trust your own feelings and judgment. If you don't believe what your partner just did in REHEARSAL, that disbelief becomes a stimulus to which you respond. Express your genuine response through the lines of the TEXT. If you stay on a level of TRUTH, you will force your partner onto the same level if he is to communicate effectively with you. Be careful. When you encounter your partner faking tears and you don't buy it, deal with what's real, her *faking* is real not the tears. Express yourself in terms of why are you faking crying? or that strategy won't work with me, only don't say it explicitly. Say it implicitly. Express your true feelings through tone and gesture, using the playwright's words.

There are times when we just get lazy and give in to a partner's shortcuts. There are times when we may set up a partner to collude with us. Be vigilant. Be responsible. Your creative work is a reflection and expression of your SOUL, don't sell it short.

Comedy

The lighter side of drama. The dramatic components that make us laugh.

"This should be played for comedy." "Get the laughs on this section." "Do it this way or they won't laugh!" Those statements are the 'tragic flaws' of comedy. You don't play it for comedy or tragedy, you play it for TRUTH. There is a story attributed to the Lunts. In the dressing room, after a performance, Alfred Lunt said to Lynn Fontanne, "Did you see how they howled when I asked for more tea?" "Yes Alfred darling," replied Ms. Fontanne, "you were marvelous." Several weeks passed and the laughs ceased on the 'tea' line. Finally one evening after their show Mr. Lunt could no longer contain himself. "Lynn," he said, "they don't laugh on the 'tea' line any longer. I don't understand it." "Alfred dear," said Ms. Fontanne, "when you stop asking for a laugh, and start asking for the tea..."

If the situation is funny, the actor playing it will be too. Playing comedy, as in playing tragedy or drama, means playing the truth of the situation as written. It means the actor carries out the 'doings' of the CHARACTER. When an actor says or does something funny, it's because of his behavior within the context of the scene. The character is doing something. He or she is not usually trying to be funny. If the actor does try to be funny he will be doing something that the character doesn't do. In fact, when anyone tries to be funny in life, we are apt to react with a groan.

There are people who are naturally funny and are not aware of it. They're not trying to be funny. Their way of thinking and behaving follows a different logic from our own. When we suddenly come to understand that logic, we laugh.

There are also those who use humor deliberately and effectively in order to accomplish something. Their humor becomes the means of attaining their OBJECTIVE. With these people, the humor is usually a reflection of either something familiar or some other form of truth that leads the listener to see certain absurdities or incongruities that make us laugh.

Comedy is an extension of logic. You present your friend with a pie because you like him. He makes you angry. You extend the logic and hit him in the face with the pie. Most comedy exists within the writing. The scene is either written humorously or it isn't. Someone had to write, "She throws the pie!" If you ever get the chance to observe comedy writers you will see how serious many of them are. Show them a funny scene on paper, and they'll read it pensively, seriously, and impassively. Then they will look up and without so much as a hint of a smile they'll say, "That's funny."

'Playing comedy' means creating the proper inner life. Your CHOICE will determine whether you're exploiting the comedic elements of the script or not. Take, for example, any of the fighting scenes in "The Odd Couple." On the surface it appears that Felix and Oscar might hate each another. If you play it that way, your inner life becomes hostile. Hostility will not be funny. Nor is it what Neil Simon wrote. The incongruity here is that these two men are friends. There is LOVE between them. Therefore, they are not coming from a place of hostility, they're coming from a place of frustration. The more frustrated they become, the angrier they can get, and the funnier the scene will be.

The actor pursues the same ACTIONS as the character. If the character is trying to win in a competitive scene, he takes actions that will accomplish his goal. He will not forego the action for the result.

There is also the question of timing. With timing there is good news and bad news. The good news is that timing helps you to focus your actions and INTENTIONS so there is no misunderstanding your character. Timing gives the audience and your partner a chance to 'get' what's happening. The bad news is, it can't be taught. If you want to be funny in a scene, find the love in the scene first, then fight like hell to maintain the love and get what you need. Once you've accomplished that, remember—timing is everything!

There is a sad belief that good, so-called straight actors may not be good comedic actors, and good dramatic actors may 'not be right' for comedy. This is extremely limited thinking. It has more to do with the business of TYPE casting than a belief that it's true. Milton Berle and Buddy Hackett are accomplished actors, comedic and dramatic. Robert De Niro and Meryl Streep have been funny in movies. If you can act, you can act drama and you can act comedy. No joke!

Concentration
The ability or act of focusing all your attention or energy where you want or need it.

Concentration, or the ability to focus, single-mindedly, seems the most necessary of all the tools for any artist or craftsperson. You don't have to deal with it directly though. That's not to say it isn't a vital component of the work. It obviously is. However, consider the possibility that your lack of concentration (assuming, of course, you feel you have a lack of concentration) may be due to the result of a small CHOICE. If you take a risk and make a strong, personal choice, that choice has a very real and SPECIFIC meaning to you, and you will not lose your concentration.

Imagine that your OBJECTIVE is to get a puppy to stay still. You can impose a set of harnesses and leashes on the animal to physically restrict its movement, or you can supply a bowl of the puppy's favorite food. The food is obviously the simpler choice as it will make the puppy *want* to stay still.

STANISLAVSKI trained actors to concentrate by using a 'circle of attention' consisting of a small 'circle of light'. Students would focus their powers of observation on everything that was within the circle and then the circle would be systematically enlarged. Ultimately, the circle could be as large as the stage in the theatre, the theatre itself, even the beach and the ocean, bounded only by the horizon.

If concentration is a problem, it is an indication that you are not paying attention. Where does your mind *want* to go? Could you be avoiding something that frightens you? Discover what happens when you try to concentrate. Does tension creep into your muscles? Do you shake your leg or drum your fingers? These are symptoms of relying on a choice that isn't really INVOLVING you.

Try this: count, in your head or out loud, one, two, three, four, five, six, seven, eight, none, ten, eleven, twelve, thirteen, fourteen, fifteen. What happened? Did your eyes take in the numbers as a whole because you knew what was between one and fifteen? Did you rush to get it over with? Maybe you *did* count slowly. Were all the numbers correct? No, they weren't! Did you notice the mistake? 'None' instead of 'nine'. What other thoughts did you have? Place your hand on a spot on the wall at 9:13 PM tomorrow and keep it there for two minutes. Can you do it? Will you? Can you spend the two minutes focused on one thing? Can you come up with a good, personal reason why you might want or need to keep your finger on the spot for two minutes?

Years ago TV commercials used to be a full minute. Now they're more likely to be thirty seconds or even fifteen seconds. But it won't be fifteen seconds of one thing. No, it will be as many cuts, or edits as they can jam in. They already know your mind *wants* to wander. That's how they make *you* concentrate on *their* product.

Craft
A collection of mastered techniques, designed to enhance, express, and develop artistic talent.

If you talk to enough actors, work with enough directors, and read enough books and articles on acting, one word keeps emerging as most important—craft.

Among the meanings of 'craft' defined by Webster's are: an occupation or trade requiring...artistic skill and skill in deceiving to gain an end. The latter sounds theatrical, doesn't it? The word 'craft' came from Middle English and Old High German. It meant strength. Theatrically speaking, craft is the difference between potential and fulfillment. Having a craft you can trust is a prerequisite to being an artist.

Harold Clurman moderating the Playwrights/Directors Unit at the Actors Studio, asserted, "I'm not interested in actors, I'm interested in craftsmen!" For a while I was perplexed on hearing this. What I really was, was scared that as an actor I didn't have a craft. Well, as I studied and worked, I acquired one. But we still haven't defined what an artist's craft is. Here goes...

As artists, the most fundamental quality we possess is PASSION. Next comes the need and desire to express our passion to others. Some artists are so gifted they appear to do it naturally. "Never took a lesson!" we hear parents proclaim proudly. Eventually, as we pursue our dreams, we run up against OBSTACLES. We learn techniques that will help us to overcome the obstacles. As we learn and collect these techniques in our tool kit, we can achieve our goals more easily. We can achieve more, period. We have developed within ourselves the resources to accomplish TASKS that, without these tools, we couldn't do. We can now share our passions, our ideas, and our thoughts more immediately. Our influence is greater and we have the opportunity to turn passion into art that can cause change.

If just one person has his or her mind changed as the result of a shared artistic passion, whether it is an actor's performance, the product of a playwright, or the concept of a director, these changes can overlap into society and industry to bring about changes that can affect the world. Developing your craft is casting a vote for yourself and the world you live in.

Critique
Honest feedback on your work. What did work, what didn't, what we saw and what we didn't see.

A critique is the product of a critic. When we become critics, we are expressing to an artist what we saw or experienced in order to help the artist. Therefore, a good critique should leave the person who's up there feeling that he's been helped.

There are classes and workshops that allow the participants to give a critique, and there are classes and workshops where only the teacher or director critiques the actor.

Critiquing is part of your business. If you can critique someone else, you will be more acute with your own work. As a part of business it should be *un*emotional. Emotion is counter productive to business. If an actor has made a CHOICE or played a part in a way that makes you angry, do both of you a favor and keep your mouth shut. If, however, you know the actor has worked for being DRUNK and headachy, you *can* and should tell him whether or not you saw that.

If you have an idea or an insight into what the artist is struggling to achieve, share it with him. Although the word critique is related to critic, it doesn't mean that what you say must be negatively critical. In fact, if you say it in a negative or a destructive way, you might cause the artist to tense up, close off, and become an adversary. At that point it doesn't matter whether you're right or not. You're not being heard. If you see that the actor has accomplished his objective successfully, then tell him that in a positive critique.

Cue
A predetermined signal to cause you to act, deliver a line, do stage business, gesture, or move on stage. A prompt.

Your cue is the signal that begins your acting journey. A cue is technical. It is something the actor deals with, whether or not in CHARACTER. There are sound cues, light cues, music cues, scene change, and curtain cues. The stage manager gives most of the cues, but cues can be taken from another actor, either by what he says or does.

It is important to translate your cues from technical to artistic ACTIONS. If your cue is the end of an actor's speech, a change in lights, a particular piece of music or a sound effect, weave it into the fabric of your PREPARATION if you can. Make your actions the result of a stimulus originating from the play. You want your audience to see you enter from your character's *need to do so*, not because someone provided a cue.

There are, also, scripts called 'cue scripts'. Please read the entries on SHAKESPEARE and VERSE TECHNIQUE for further discussion regarding cue scripts.

Cues are obviously vital to any collaborative theatrical endeavor. Without them we could not function artistically. In other words, cues are not to be missed.

Down Stage
The part of a proscenium stage that is closest to the audience.

There was a time when stages were literally pitched at an angle or raked, so that the audience could see better. Down stage was actually at the bottom of the 'hill' nearest the audience. This is still the case in many theatres. Set pieces are constructed accordingly. A table, for instance, will have the rear legs cut shorter so that the tabletop will be level when it sits on an inclined stage. See UP STAGE.

Emotional Memory

Exploring, or creating a past event from your life for use in a scene or character. Also called emotional recall or affective memory.

STANISLAVSKI first termed this memory of emotion. The inspiration for it came from the work of Dr. Theodule Ribot, a French psychologist[1] who did some clinical work in this area. From the very beginning Dr. Ribot used the terms AFFECTIVE MEMORY and emotional memory interchangeably.

One method director and teacher, who shall remain nameless, maintains there is a difference between affective memory and emotional memory. Affective memory, he claims, is the sensory (SENSE MEMORY) recollection of an event that affects you with the emotions that you may not have expressed at the actual event, while emotional memory is the straight expression of an event from the past. In other words, if you create the sensory events of your dog dying and you cry in the present, without having cried at the actual event in the past, that constitutes an affective memory. However, if you did cry then and you do cry now, that's an emotional memory, or an EMOTIONAL RECALL. Honestly, the discussion can quickly become specious.

Use the technique to help EXPLORE the origins of your unique behavior and to help create an origin for the behaviors you will use in your work so that your work is genuinely ORGANIC. There are actors who can push an emotional button and cry, get angry, or laugh on command. When we watch these actors in a scene, we will find ourselves coming out of the play to marvel at their real tears, their production of emotion (emoting), and so

---

[1] La Psychologie des Sentiments, 1896 and later Problèmes de Psychologie Affective, 1910

on. Whereas, when an actor is organic, we will empathize with the CHARACTER; we stay involved in the play because we understand and feel the sequence of events that led to the behavior we're seeing.

Emotional Recall

Exploring, or creating a past event from your life for use in a scene or character. Also called emotional memory or affective memory.

See AFFECTIVE MEMORY and EMOTIONAL MEMORY.

Endowment

To assign specific attributes and/or idiosyncrasies to objects and/or other people.

How are you handling and relating physically to this book right now? It's a simple, paperback book. You just bought it, or someone lent or gave you his copy. Do you place the book, still open, face down to hold your place when you stop reading? Do you fold the corner of a page down instead of using a bookmark? Do you highlight or underline certain sections for later reference? Do you think twice about writing in it? In pen or pencil? When you lift the book, how much do your arm muscles tell you it weighs? The answers to these and many other questions about how you deal with this book will be vastly different if you endow the book with the properties of say an original edition of the 1597 quarto of Shakespeare's *The Tragedy of Romeo and Juliet*. If you have the chance to handle a very rare and valuable object, you will see how differently you treat the object. You might handle it more slowly, more carefully and even notice changes in your breathing.

The difference between handling a valuable antique and an everyday item can also be perceived as a difference in circumstances (see GIVEN CIRCUMSTANCES).

You can take any tangible object and endow it with properties that you want it to have, then behave accordingly. A ring from a Cracker Jacks box can be endowed with the attributes of your great grandmother's diamond wedding ring for example.

To be accurate and ORGANIC in applying endowment to your acting, you should understand SENSE MEMORY. The sensory work will enable your senses to respond viscerally to the instructions in your endowment. Sensory will also help you believe the circumstances.

If you can endow an object, you can endow a person. If you're having difficulty RELATING to your partner, try endowing him with characteristics of people from your life to whom you can relate. See also, AS IF, PERSONALIZATION, and SUBSTITUTION.

Sometimes the wave in a persons hair, or the shape of her eyebrows, or maybe the timbre of her voice will remind you of someone. By focusing specifically on those aspects, you can use them to create a character in the other actor who has a personal meaning to you.

It is said that when Winston Churchill would address an audience and he was nervous, he would endow the audience members with nakedness. If that wasn't enough he would then see them naked and sitting on the toilet. If you are doing the endowing, then the possibilities are limited only by your IMAGINATION. Have fun!

Energy
The vitality that is evidenced in your performance.

"Energy can be neither created nor destroyed," said Albert Einstein, yet thousands of acting teachers and directors still continue to harangue actors to "create more energy" in their scenes. When a director says that you or the scene needs more energy, you need to translate that into terms that will allow you to make CHOICES yielding that result. And make no mistake about it, energy is the result of a process.

The energy is already within you. It's what to tell yourself in order to release it that becomes important. The size of your choice will determine the amount of energy you release. If you tell yourself you're in love with him, you will have more energy than believing he's just a nice guy.

Physically you can increase your energy output immediately by PROJECTING, or talking louder. You can also move with more authority by using more physical space. All of these choices must be SPECIFICALLY MOTIVATED and JUSTIFIED.

The behavioral choices you make will determine the quantity and quality of your energy.

Environment
The ability to create accurately the characters surroundings.

When we go to the theatre, we may see scenes that take place on top of the Statue of Liberty, a fifteenth century castle, or out at sea. The actor, to help tell the story effectively, must convey the environmental essence of the scene as well as the other obligations necessary in creating theatrical TRUTH.

The actor must do the HOMEWORK necessary to create the environment for the audience and for himself to transport us back in time properly, out to sea, etc. See PLACE and SENSE-MEMORY.

Exploration
All the different choices and ideas you try in rehearsal to arrive at a performance.

Can you imagine reading who the CHARACTER is, seeing what he does and then just doing that and no more? You could end up with a performance that is flat, with no color or originality. No uniqueness. No surprises!

Exploration is the process of wondering, questioning, and investigating different ways of doing something. It could be finding different ways of achieving your OBJECTIVES or of pursuing your ACTIONS. It could be examining different MANNERISMS, ACCENTS, or clothing CHOICES. If you allow yourself to question and be curious, rather than simply answer and play, you will have a character with depth and dimension. You will bring someone to the stage with a full life. Your behavior will be exciting to watch because the audience can identify with and believe in a multi-faceted person.

When you see a brilliant performance on the stage, in the movies, or on television and you say, "Who would have ever thought to do that, or say that line that way?" the secret is that the actor didn't think about it either. He didn't figure it out intellectually. The result you saw came from his total belief in what was around him and what he was doing. There was a real need to accomplish, to strive, to achieve an objective. Because he was INVOLVED, he found INSTINCTIVE ways of doing things that were often different from what we 'thought' they would or should do. He did what he believed worked best to get what he wanted.

When you set out to explore (REHEARSE), think in terms of cause and effect. Think stimulus/response. Then you will be within the guidelines of nature.

Stanislavski asked, "What would *I* do if *I* were the character in this situation?" If I'm playing Hamlet and I'm seeking revenge, what is it that I do? How do I behave when I want revenge? True, that gets you off to a start by looking at different responses to the same stimulus, however, a more thorough and more accurate question to pose is one later set forth by a student of Stanislavski's named Evgeny Vakhtangov. Vakhtangov's 'reformulation' was, "What would I have to do in order to do what the character does in this situation?" In other words, as Hamlet, "What would I, as an actor, have to do to create what Hamlet does, what *he* believes in?"

Let's say you've tried everything and still nothing is happening, Strasberg advised, "Start from zero." In other words start just from where you are in the MOMENT. Even if, in your judgment, it has nothing to do with the character or the situation. You will be beginning at a level of TRUTH. If you start out on a truthful level, you can build more truth on your foundation of truth.

External Work
The technical part of the work that pertains to "selling" your performance, irrespective of emotions, behavior, or internal work.

External work, in New York City Method parlance always seemed to be a 'put-down' of a way to approach acting.

American actors work internally, from the inside out. English actors, like the late Lord Olivier, work externally, from the outside in. American actors usually think of the external British approach as too broad and 'stagey.' Whereas the British think much of our American acting is too 'mumbly', small, or self indulgent.

When you go to London to see theatre for yourself, you'll be wowed! The only plays on the West End you may not like might be American productions. The English are clearly doing something different from what we Americans have been taught. There is a broadness to it, whatever that means. It is also 'stagey' in a way—no, theatrical would be a better word. Yet it is unmistakably TRUTHFUL.

As one learns more about the British approach, one begins to see how unproductive and silly it is for one side or the other to be THE way to work. Instead of each side putting down the other, perhaps there is a way to take the best from both approaches and weave them together for an even stronger fabric than just one way by itself.

When directors AUDITION actors, they often see personal, full commitment work, yet it's not theatrical in the positive sense of the word. Actors don't know how to do an exit line, or where the strongest points on the stage are. They don't know how to find their light and many don't use their bodies well. They also don't have a viable approach to breaking down the TEXT.

When Lawrence Olivier began his process by working out what kind of nose his CHARACTER had, it ultimately lead to a balance of external and INTERNAL WORK. There are Brits, however, who maintain that it is sheer nonsense to have to 'feel it' in order to play it.

STANISLAVSKI devotes much of his writings on the 'system' to external work covering such areas as plasticity, which was a fluidity of movement.

The bottom line must be that regardless of how you approach the work, it's the audience who is the final arbiter of whether or not it has witnessed the truth.

Fourth Wall
The invisible, imagined, or implied wall through which the audience sees the performance.

There are several thoughts on what the fourth wall is. Commonly, it is the imagined wall between the actors and the audience. It is located on the apron[1] of the stage in a PROSCENIUM theatre.

---

[1] Apron: The edge of the stage that is closest to the audience. The part of the stage that is farthest DOWN STAGE.

When the set is a typical living room, the audience sees the UP STAGE, back wall and the STAGE RIGHT and STAGE LEFT walls respectively. The audience is then asked to imagine the fourth wall.

When playing a scene, actors will make SPECIFIC CHOICES in order to create the fourth wall for themselves and their audiences. An actor and/or director might place an imaginary mirror on the fourth wall. As the actor creates the mirror, he also creates the fourth wall. Some scenes require the CHARACTERS to look at paintings. These paintings are frequently imaginary as well. Where do you hang an imaginary painting? On an imaginary wall.

The problem with the fourth wall concept is with theatrical metaphor and theatrical ENERGY. In the metaphor, we will believe we are seeing into a living room, an office, a castle, etc. With energy however, the actor must extend it past the fourth wall. His energy must, of necessity, reach the back row of the audience. Therefore the fourth wall can be thought of as actually being behind the audience.

Thousands of years ago, storytellers, lyric poets, and actors addressed the audience directly. This was always truthful because actors and audiences were always equally lit. Performances were done in the afternoon or out of doors. At the turn of the nineteenth century, theatres began installing Edison's new electric lights. Prior to this, even though performances were held in the evening using candles, gas lights, and lime lights, the audience was still lit, along with the actors, by those beautiful old theatre chandeliers. With the advent of electric light it became too expensive to light the audience. Actors, for the first time in theatrical history couldn't see the audience. So instead of facing out and talking to people they couldn't see very well, they turned to speak to each other. It was at this point that playwrights began writing more naturalistic or realistic plays. The fourth wall in this respect is really a wall of theatrical light.

Gear Changes
Theatricalizing the variances or differences in a body of text.

When I first heard the British acting term gear changes, I thought is was one of those quaint English expressions. It isn't. It is a great technique. It isn't the same as ACTION either.

Between the beginning and end of one action you might have many gear changes. Just as a car continues travelling in the same direction, there may be several gear changes based on the many hills, climate changes like icy roads, or shifts in speed.

Gear changes are particularly effective should you become aware that you're playing on one emotional level; or put another way, when you're expressing only one color.

If you have only had METHOD style training and are used to EXPLORING a role thoroughly, if you need to find only ORGANIC reasons to express a line as you feel it, you have two options: skip this section, or keep an open mind. Find a private place and try out the technique alone. If you find it works, you then must MOTIVATE all your 'gear-change' CHOICES. That is, create a stimulus for your character to say the line that way. When you learn that you can use what you've found, simply don't tell anyone. If you're ready to give this a try, proceed with caution but make certain you have fun.

Start by simply deciding on some gear changes, or variations of how you might express your lines. This really is a simple, EXTERNAL technique.

"To be, or not to be. That is the question." Say the line. Is it one color? Yes? Then add two gear changes. Say in a pensive voice, "To be, or not to be." Now change gears. Using an emphatic tone continue with, "That is the question." Or, add three gear changes. Try "To be," said very quickly, then very slowly say, "or not to be." Now playing strong irony, "That is the question." Or, instead of irony, just say it quieter. Are these choices correct? Who cares! Again, it is simply an external technique (nothing to do with emotions or behavior) that allows you to build levels into your performance technically. Experiment. Try many different gear changes in your REHEARSALS.

In class, a lot of actors unwittingly PATTERN their lines. No matter what choices they make, the RHYTHM, cadence, and inflection of their lines never change. There are some INTERNAL, behavioral exercises that can help, but, if actors are going to pattern their lines instinctively, then why not pattern them in a way that not only tells the story the author wrote, but also makes it easier and more fun to act..

In rehearsal for a new comedy, an actress had the lines "No, no". Most of us would just say "No, no", and that would be that. In context, the boy had just been slapped by the girl he was in love with. He questioned her with "Is it that women's thing?" She answered, "No, no..." and continued with her explanation. The actress added a gear change between No and no. This is what happened:

He: "Is it that women's thing?"
She: (In a simple, innocent tone) "No," then,
     as the real meaning of the question
     dawned on her, with a combination of
     embarrassment and indignation she said,
     "*NO!*"

The audience howled. The actress loved that moment each time she played it. She simply added a gear change, made the choice and then she motivated it.

Next time a director, teacher or even your own voice tells you that you're playing it on one level, or it's one color emotionally, try shifting gears and see how much easier it can be to get from here to there.

Gibberish (numbers, letters, etc.)
A technique using non-verbal sounds in place of the text or in place of words.

Gibberish is a classic technique to help actors express their true feelings with out being influenced by the intellectual content of the lines or, if it's an *improvisation* or an exercise, thinking of what to say next.

When you've made a strong CHOICE and you have committed to an emotional PREPARATION, you can access pure truthful behavior by expressing no more or less than what you're feeling in gibberish.

Create for yourself sensorily that it's really hot and humid outside and you're going to call it quits with your lover. When you express behavior using the lines, does the little, internalized director inhibit you from expressing all that you're really feeling? Or do you sense that what you've got isn't enough, and so you do a little more, just for some insurance?

Either way you're compromising the integrity of your genuine MOMENT TO MOMENT behavior. The problem is that when you read the line, you know in your head what it means. That intellectual knowledge can color your delivery by serving as a director. The little director in you says, "Don't say what you're feeling, say the line according to what you think is happening now."

Try gibberish instead: numbers or letters of the alphabet said randomly. There is a logical way to say a line of text for intellectual meaning. But there is no logical way to say a string of numbers: "Fourteen, twenty six, a hundred and nine, twelve, ten, three thousand and seven." It's going to come out as purely as you feel it.

In our classes and workshops we tend to use numbers more than gibberish. Some actors become inhibited at the idea of having to say silly, nonsensical words. It's just plain easier to say "fifteen" than it is to say "oozie-whattle-dumploink".

As actors, you're paid to help the author and director tell a story to the audience. You do it through the creation of behavior and the expression of sounds in the form of the playwright's words. To express the sounds of just the pure behavior, use gibberish. To go from gibberish to words, use numbers. After all, fifteen is a word, but there is no logical, intellectual way to act it. It only comes out the way you feel in the moment. Once you're expressing gibberish or numbers and you hook into the behavior, go to the words of the play. If you should start to lose the behavior and you try to make sense of the words, go back to gibberish. You will once again hear only the truth. It's a great way to teach your INSTRUMENT to tell the truth.

EXERCISE

You and a friend agree to tell each other the most intimate details of your love life. You agree to speak in gibberish or random numbers.

1. How much did you learn about using gibberish/numbers?

2. About your friend's love life?

Given Circumstances

The information in the play set down for you by the playwright.

"Romeo, Romeo. Wherefore art thou, Romeo?" says Juliet, on her balcony,[1] at night. The playwright has given you the circumstances. It's night. She's on a balcony (PLACE) and higher than he. She loves him. He loves her. And another bit of useful given circumstance is that she can't see him because it's dark. Perhaps you disagree with the last statement. All you need to do is play the scene both ways; she *can* see him and then, she *can't*. See which one plays better theatrically.

Regardless, what you do with your circumstances is your business as an artist. You make your own CHOICES. But to ignore them or overlook them is to risk deviating from telling the story the playwright wrote.

Given circumstances are clues as to how to make choices, how to PREPARE, and how to seek out OBSTACLES. The more circumstances you can identify, the more choices you can make, execute, and express.

How do you identify the given circumstances? Look first at the physical circumstances. Is the scene in or out of doors? What is the weather and how does it affect the

---

[1] According to Shakespeare's First Folio (1623) there is no mention of Juliet being on a balcony. In another scene the Folio specifies 'aloft', it doesn't say a balcony. It was the Italian custom, in the sixteenth century (extant quartos of R & J were dated 1597), to have the bed chambers on the second floor. Juliet could therefore appear in a second story window. Also, according to pictures we have of Elizabethan theatres, there were windows in the dressing room upstage. A convenient place to play the scene from 'aloft.'

CHARACTERS and the scene? In what historical period does the play take place? How does your period costume change or affect your ACTIONS? Your PHYSICAL ACTIONS? Question the events in your character's past and your character's psychological make up. All these circumstances will affect your choices of actions and OBJECTIVES.

When Stella Adler[1] went to meet STANISLAVSKI in Paris because she was having difficulties with his 'system', he spent weeks privately coaching her in the use of given circumstances. "The truth in art," said Stanislavksi, "is the truth of your circumstances."

Homework

The work that you do for yourself before class, rehearsals, or performance.

Have you always hated homework? You probably hated being embarrassed even more though. And that's what happens if you don't do your homework.

After you have sleuthed out the clues in the text from GIVEN CIRCUMSTANCES, CHARACTER RELATIONSHIPS, ACTIONS and OBJECTIVES, you need to make some CHOICES to find out what works and what doesn't. While it's true that the place to do that is in REHEARSAL, there is much to be accomplished on your own, before your first rehearsal.

Sometimes there are SENSORY clues in the play. The scene might be set in a sweltering jungle, or you might be freezing on a mountain top. These circumstances can and should be created and worked on at home.

---

[1]   Stella Adler was a student of Stanislavski and an original member of The Group Theatre in the 1930s. The Group Theatre revolutionized American theatre with powerful, realistic plays and performances. Stella Adler was one of the finest actors and teachers in America. She founded the Stella Adler Conservatory of Acting in 1949.

Also reading the play several times will constantly reveal new clues to EXPLORE. That also constitutes homework.

Many actors plot out in their scripts the beginning and end of each action and make personal notes on the TRANSITIONS from one action to another.

Research is homework. Once an actor played a furniture refinisher in a television drama. As part of his homework, he found a real furniture refinisher and volunteered to help him in his job, just to find elements of authenticity. He found that they both would pick their fingernails continuously to get bits of dried varnish out. That became a choice for a MANNERISM. He learned how the chemicals affected his breathing and how to use the tools professionally. This is all homework. It is not for rehearsal.

Homework is also the literal assignment you get in class. It might be a scene assignment or a sensory TASK. Either way, the more you do, the more you will become committed to your part.

Homework in SENSE MEMORY is essential for the learning to take place. In any of the sense memory exercises in this book, homework is the one element that will insure success. Sensorily speaking, you need to put in about an hour a day for one week on your sensory task before bringing it into the studio for class. During that week's worth of homework you are EXPLORING all the facets of how your senses relate and respond to the stimuli you're dealing with.

Some classes don't assign homework, and it makes the learning and understanding more difficult, to say the least. Once you realize that and take time out at home to work systematically on your OBJECT for about an hour a day, you can bring into class some real work for a thorough CRITIQUE.

This homework *is* the work.

Imaginary Monologue
A monologue you create yourself, spur of the moment, and express to an imaginary (or sensorily created) person.

An imaginary monologue is a useful tool or exercise to help you access genuine behavior when the logic of a part interferes with the TRUTH.

First, create a person with whom you have a significant emotional connection. Create the person using SENSE MEMORY, not just your IMAGINATION. Then express all the things that might be difficult if that person were really standing before you.

There will be a flow of expressive behavior that automatically contains within it an OBJECTIVE, an ACTION, RELATIONSHIP and a PREPARATION. It is real and it will bring elements to a MONOLOGUE or SCENE that may never have been found without making the emotional commitment that this exercise accomplishes.

Imagination
That part of the mind that allows for the creation of images to bring us closer to solving a problem or to express more fully our true nature.

Imagination may be the single most important component in the act of creation or why it is that we need to express ourselves as actors. It is a magic door from the concrete to the abstract. It is the pathway to pure creativity. It is the repository of all our dreams and all the answers. It is also the highest form of personal entertainment. It only makes sense to draw upon it and share it, publicly, in special rooms. Receiving acknowledgment from those with whom we share ourselves in a fusion of feelings and ideas, unites us in passion and validates the human experience. It is another way of saying theatre.

To use imagination in our work as artists, it is important to remember that imagination, like its product ideas, cannot be forced or ordered on demand. Rather it must be allowed, cultivated, and encouraged to happen.

Sometimes directors talk to their casts about "making the magic". But how do you make magic? The answer is—I'm not sure you can. But you can set the conditions for magic to happen. That is what PREPARATION and RELAXATION contribute to. The rule, if it can be called that, is to leave yourself alone. Don't push anything. Trust your CRAFT and trust yourself. Keep yourself open and in a state of wonder. Find the LOVE in every CHARACTER, in every SCENE and, most importantly, in yourself. Continually look to express your best self and you will walk through the portals of creativity.

Imagine that!

Immediacy

A quality to be strived for in making your work look like and exist in the present. Also, technique designed to justify a faster pace.

When Cinderella falls in love with the Prince she wants to spend the rest of her life with him, but she has to leave before midnight or...you know what will happen. That 'you know what' business, theatrically speaking, creates an immediacy. An immediacy is a JUSTIFICATION for faster, or more animated behavior.

Let's say you're doing a play where your CHARACTER wants to avoid a confrontation with the other characters. You can choose an immediacy to get away from them quickly. Let's also say that the TEXT says you don't feel too well. Using SENSE MEMORY you might create nausea and a need to throw up. You certainly didn't want to throw up in front of anyone. That CHOICE will compel you to move much faster and more believably in terms of your character than just deciding to go faster.

In employing an immediacy, care should be taken to make choices that parallel the logic of the scene. If, for instance, you choose an immediacy that involves a bomb going off five minutes after the scene starts, then the audience is going to wonder what's wrong with you if the play doesn't explain so-called 'bomb behavior' later. Or worse, the audience won't be able to follow the ACTION.

Another use of the term 'immediacy' is a description of the work in the present. It means you are not AN-TICIPATING. You're working MOMENT TO MOMENT. The scene doesn't look REHEARSED, it looks like it's happening for the very first time. It's happening right now. It has a certain immediacy to it.

Improvisation
An unrehearsed scene, in your own, extemporaneous words.

Improvs, as they are usually referred to, are unrehearsed scenes that you cowrite with your partner and without pen and paper.

The main thing to keep in mind is that an improv is a tool used to solve a particular problem.

Directors can learn a lot about an actor by suggesting an improv, either about a SPECIFIC SCENE or a certain CHARACTER, in an AUDITION.

As a means of exploring character MOTIVATIONS and behavior, improvs can often be a shortcut . One goal of a scene is to make it look spontaneous. It should appear to be happening for the first time. When you abandon the TEXT and find out about your own IMPULSES within the context of the GIVEN CIRCUMSTANCES of the scene, you are teaching your INSTRUMENT and your character the very spontaneity you're seeking. This is invaluable in REHEARSAL. It is one of the best tools around to help an actor EXPLORE.

Improvisation used in class is also great for teaching new actors to stay INVOLVED in what they have created for themselves and, at the same time, develop naturalistic or truthful behavior. Since improvisation is based on following impulses, it is helpful to get actors out of their heads and into their guts. When that is accomplished the audience can participate, not just observe. It can feel with the character on a gut level.

When the above work is assimilated, the skill of improvisation can really pay off in performance itself.

A wonderful moment occurred in the Broadway production of *Dinner At Eight* with an all star cast, directed by Tyrone Guthrie. In the opening scene June Havoc was penning her invitations while talking on the telephone. From high in the balcony came some unintelligible remark from a heckler. It was audible to all in the theatre. Without missing a beat, Ms. Havoc glanced up at the area in the balcony, while also staying in character and in her PLACE, and said, "Oh no, I don't believe we'd want him!" The audience, of course, broke into applause. We should all have such successful improvs.

In the British theatre, when a mistake like the one above happens, the director will intentionally build it into the show. It will be repeated to look like an accident every night thereafter. The reason is that the audience knows that that incident didn't happen before and isn't likely to occur again, therefore it was just for them. It was special. That's exciting, and it's theatre.

Impulses
Natural causes or stimuli that can be expressed vocally and physically.

An impulse is a feeling, an instant message, telling you to take a certain action. You either do or you don't. In life you might have the impulse to kill someone. Obviously you would not act on that, you would find a more creative way to express that impulse. In acting it's good to follow your impulses. Don't let them pass in favor of working out the best way to present what's going on inside you.

Imagine that you touch a candle flame. Your impulse might be to say, "Ouch!" or whatever you might really say. But you certainly don't touch the flame, feel the pain, and then decide theatrically how best you might express "Ouch!" That would be absurd. Many actors do just that when they're working on a part, and we in the audience never get to access the actor or the CHARACTER on a feeling level.

Following your impulses is really another way of telling the TRUTH. Impulses are the manifestations of your uniqueness. They are what brings nature and life to a performance. Impulses are the very fiber of behavior. And after all, as an actor, behavior is what you're selling. Express every impulse, as it happens, in the MOMENT.

Indicating
Pointing to what behavior is supposed to look like rather than creating genuine truthful behavior.

She's supposed to cry in the SCENE, but she can't, so she puts her head in her hands, covers her face, shakes her shoulders and syncopates her speech. "She's not crying, she's indicating!" Hence the cry of the METHOD actor.

My British colleagues would not agree. They believe that you can fake it as much as you like as long as the audience believes it. Actually, if the audience does believe it, then the realists or Method practitioners wouldn't know whether or not the actor was indicating. Put another way, if the audience doesn't believe the actor or the behavior, it's just plain bad acting, irrespective of whether he or she is indicating or not.

Actors are trained to make personal CHOICES that draw from real life experience so that the behavior that results will be TRUTHFUL. In fact the crux of STANISLAVSKI'S system is to make your CHOICES based on life or nature, not on what you think might look good on the stage. An example would be an actress trying to cry because her CHARACTER is grieving for a loved one. If the choice is made from nature, then the actress would work to distance herself from the painful feelings and try to maintain her own sense of normalcy. She would try not to cry. That basic or natural conflict would create some very truthful behavior.

A short lesson entitled, "How To Sneeze!" The lesson is in six parts:

> Part One: Create facial grimaces, as if you are about to sneeze.
> Part Two: Grab a handkerchief or a tissue.
> Part Three: Create a loud cough from the throat: *CGHAAAH!*
> Part Four: Shout *CHOOO!*
> Part Five: Do Parts Three and Four at exactly the same time.
> Part Six: As you are about to replace your hanky in your pocket or purse, look at it, you know, the stuff that's supposed to be in there. Squish it around in your fingers subtly and replace it in your pocket or purse.
> Bless you! You've executed a stage sneeze.

Now if the script says the character must sneeze, and your nose doesn't itch or you don't have a cold, you better do something to allow the audience to believe your sneeze. Try the above technique. If the audience *doesn't* believe it—you're indicating!

Indicating, from a truly Method standpoint, is really showing the audience what your ACTION is instead of actually playing the action. If your character is supposed to annihilate her spouse, that's what you have got to do. Don't give the audience a token of what you're supposed to be doing, really do it.

Inner Monologue
A craft technique of expressing your real feelings between the phrases of the text.

Inner monologue is a tool that is often used by teachers and directors to diagnose acting problems. You can see what is in the actor's head by asking him or her to simply express what's going on in the MOMENT. Inner monologue will allow for ADJUSTMENTS that can put an actor back on track.

Inner monologue is by no means the monopoly of teachers and directors either. Actors can EXPLORE the work by using inner monologue to keep and encourage their own sense of TRUTH. For example, "To be, or not to be. That is the question. Whether it is nobler in the mind to suffer the slings and arrows of outrageous fortune...." That would be the MONOLOGUE. The inner monologue might be: "To be, or not to be. [How many actors have said those words over the last four hundred years? I hope I don't sound silly] That is the question. Whether it is nobler in the mind to suffer the slings and arrows [I wonder how old Shakespeare would have said that today if he knew about automatic weapons and bombs. It doesn't feel natural to talk like this. I have doubts] of outrageous fortune...."

You are quickly getting in touch with you own sense of truth. If what you're feeling and expressing isn't right for the scene, then you can change your CHOICE.

Inner monologue is also very helpful for a PREPARATION. It's like a look inside the mind. Often we will use this approach in class for a public preparation (a preparation that is done in front of the class and out loud). So many times we see actors prepare by putting their hand to their foreheads, turning their backs to us and waiting for a minute. The process looks intense as hell but doesn't usually make for a better performance. By asking the actor to do an inner monologue we can correct any choices that might take away from either the ACTION or the OBJECTIVE.

Inspiration

An impulse of intuition creating the impetus to behave in total harmony with the character.

Inspiration is the difficult-to-define element of the actor's art that caused STANISLAVSKI to create his 'system'. When we talk about 'making magic' in a performance, we are talking about inspiration. Inspiration is a home run, a touchdown, a bulls-eye. It is meeting your goal more than totally. How can something be more than total? The answer is: when you participate in something where your expectation is perfection, and what results surpasses your anticipation.

Every actor, every artist for that matter, holds within him the potential for inspiration. The METHOD, the system or technique or whatever you choose to call it, is an attempt to encourage and allow inspiration.

Stanislavski:

Everyone ought to realize that the multitude of failures occur just among those actors who do not know how to observe, create and build their creative 'now' without thinking of tomorrow. No other artist can possibly have so clear a conception of the unrepeatable fleeting moment as the actor, for the actor must in that fleeting instant of time grasp the full significance of a remark or of a sudden impulse of his intuition and promptly incorporate it in his part. Never again will he get exactly the same flash of inner illumination, for it is only in that 'now' that he has acquired all the powers that are active in him; his own personality is no longer a hindrance to him, and he has attained what is rightly called inspiration, that is to say, the harmoniously active powers of the mind and the heart, freed from all the influences of everyday life, except those given in his part.

Inspiration is part of what makes art art. It's very hard to find it if you look for it. Looking for it implies living in the future or ANTICIPATING. Because you're INVOLVED so totally in your work when it happens, you aren't aware of it; you're in the present, the 'now'. You don't find out that you've achieved it until after the fact, in the past—and usually because someone else, the audience, told you.

Instinct

The nonintellectual, or innate stimulus for action.

Instinct is something we all share. It is the natural and impulsive response we feel towards whatever stimuli we are currently experiencing.

Instinct in the theatre is what we need to get in touch with, develop, and encourage TRUTHFUL behavior. Developing healthy instincts will take you DOWN STAGE if you happen to be UP STAGING your partner. It will help you find your light on stage and get you to shift your body if you're blocking your partners light.

Instinct is a feeling or IMPULSE connected to your gut. It says, "Do this now, you must." You will usually be rewarded with the full expression of your own uniqueness if you pay attention to and act on your instinct. Developing your theatrical instinct has everything to do with trusting your CRAFT.

Instrument

You.

You. Your body, Your voice, and, I add to that, your mind and your SOUL. Why soul? STANISLAVSKI continuously referred to the soul as a vital component of his system. It is that aspect of your commitment that places your imprimatur on your work. It is what makes your performance uniquely you.

If a pianist's instrument is the piano, the actor's instrument is himself. It is therefore crucial that as actors we keep our instruments finely tuned, both physically and mentally, so that we may fully respond to any stimulus that occurs.

Intention
What you and/or your character will do.

Intentions, ACTIONS and OBJECTIVES are terms that are often used interchangeably. Literally it is what the actor or the CHARACTER intends to do.

The standard teaching is to find a verb, an action word, a word that you can act. But it doesn't stop there. Intentions, actions, and objectives must have what STANISLAVSKI called through action.

Through action is a series of actions that are connected to each other and that ultimately lead to what the character wants or wants to do from the beginning of the play straight on through to end. It is what Stanislavski called the SUPER-OBJECTIVE. I don't see how actors can choose actions and objectives in a random fashion and still expect to be telling the story of the play accurately.

I assume that you will, of course, deal with the concept of the super objective when working out your intentions.

Internal work
The part of the work that deals with feelings and emotions in order to create truthful behavior.

Internal work, as stated above, has to do with your own feelings and emotions. It uses your feelings to create behavior that dramatizes the CHARACTER'S conflict. Creating TRUTHFUL believable behavior is part of what actors get paid to do.

Most teachers and directors focus much, if not all, of their emphasis on internal work; it's that important. It's what directors, agents, and casting directors look for in an audition. But internal work is not everything.

Internal work, according to Stanislavski and to common sense, must be balanced with EXTERNAL WORK. What good does it do to pour out your heart and SOUL to an audience if it doesn't reach beyond the third row of the house, or worse, if the audience doesn't understand it?

Internal work is best EXPLORED in a class or workshop where a positive supportive environment encourages you to risk expressing what you're feeling to give an audience the full depth of the character.

Involvement
The result of a full commitment to your part and your character.

When you're working properly and you're connected to your CHOICES and your partner, you are said to be involved. If you're playing an emotional scene and you're wondering whether your friends in the audience will like you, you are not involved. All of the INTERNAL techniques that form your CRAFT are fundamentally designed to involve you in the life of the CHARACTER and the TRUTH of the play.

Justification
The reason you and/or your character take an action.

Whenever you take an ACTION the audience must sense a real reason for it. Also, having a real justification for doing something will make it easier to act the part. Conversely, if you're having some difficulty in playing a particular role, try looking to see if you've done your HOMEWORK with regard to justifying your CHARACTER'S actions.

Think in terms of cause and effect, or stimulus/response. If the GIVEN CIRCUMSTANCES of the play require a certain response or effect, then ask what the cause or stimulus is that generates that response. If your director says, "Pick up the PACE!" do you simply move and say your lines faster and with more ENERGY, or do you give yourself a logical reason for your character to speed up? If I'm running late for an important appointment, then I have a strong reason to get moving. Maybe I'm going to throw up. CHOICES for justification might have nothing to do with the given circumstances. If Juliet is excited at the prospect of Romeo's arrival, she might just as well use her real life crush on the actor playing Romeo. If it's there, use it.

Whatever your justification is, it should follow the logic of the scene. It shouldn't be some arbitrary idea used to solve an immediate problem.

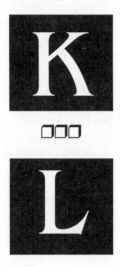

Line Readings
Instructions on how to read or say a line.

To give line readings or not to give line readings? That is the question. Many actors feel terrible or get angry when they get a line reading. They feel it is insulting or reflects a failure on their part to get it right.

Many directors, especially if they were actors first, avoid ever giving an actor a line reading for the above reasons. The reason is that it cuts out the need for a process. If you trust the process, you'll get the right answer, right? Wrong, for one simple reason. Acting technique, or process, is based in science. You have cause and effect and stimulus/response, deep breathing and progressive muscle relaxation. These elements form the scientific bases for acting but they are only a base. Acting is still and always will be an art. It is a medium that uses feelings, emotions, fantasy, ACTION, logic, and IMAGINATION to communicate an ethereal TRUTH, a laugh, a pain, or LOVE. There is no one way. Never! Well, almost never.

Sometimes a line, often in a comedy, only works if it's said one way. There really aren't any CHOICES if you're going to represent the playwright. When Henny Youngman says, "Take my wife...please!" he's saying the line in the one way that will convey the meaning that he wants. If an actor says, "Take my wife please" or "Take my wife...please" or even "Take my wife please"... well, you get the idea. The question is, what happens when the process doesn't give you the right answer? What do you do? Ask for a line reading! If you're a director, give a line reading! A secure actor will welcome a line reading if it means he can get back to the business of creating quicker.

Once, while directing one of my favorite actors in a drama, I could see he didn't understand a certain point by the way he said the line. I outlined actions, INTENTIONS, choices, and ideas for him to understand better what we were after. Finally he looked at me and said, "Hey, just give me a reading." I did and he said, "Oh, I see. Great!" and he did it, perfectly.

The bottom line: sometimes you *have* to have line readings. *You* have to have line readings. You have to *have* line readings. You have to have line *readings*.

Line Rehearsal
A rehearsal specifically for running lines.

When actors have been EXPLORING and REHEARSING a play for a few weeks, it becomes necessary to return to the basic script. That is when the director will call for a line rehearsal. The director will also call for a line rehearsal if the actors simply need to learn their lines better.

As actors investigate and explore different CHOICES in their work, they will often wander astray of the original ideas and INTENTIONS of the play. Things that worked well in the very first reading are not working now. A line rehearsal helps to get back to the original source.

It is usual in a line rehearsal to just read the play with no PAUSES for business (STAGE BUSINESS) or BLOCKING. All of a sudden the play seems to work again. The actor can now refocus his exploration of the role.

Love
"What's love got to do, got to do with it?"—Tina Turner. "Love makes the world go 'round."—Doris Day.

Love is a fact of life. Therefore love is a fact in any SCENE you wish to be lifelike. Every human being needs love.

We want it, we seek it, and we demand it. We try to give it and take it. Love becomes a kind of grand stimulus for grand responses.

If you don't think that love is a vital factor in your scene, think again. Look for it; it's there.

If you're playing a CHARACTER whom you feel is devoid of love, that may involve the lack of love. EXPLORE whether your character received love at one time or lost love, found love, or threw it away. Ask yourself who your character loves and who loves your character. When a scene is obviously a love scene, examine the absence of love (OPPOSITES).

In an art and a business where MOTIVATION, JUSTIFICATION and PHYSICAL ACTIONS are all important, allow love to be the first step in your quest to learn about your character and yourself in relation to it. There are all types of love, educate yourself about them.

Every scene is a love scene!

Mannerisms
Physical behaviors or 'ticks' pinpointing the uniqueness of the character.

Mannerisms are instant ways of communicating who to an audience the CHARACTER is. Mannerisms are also a lot of fun for actors to use.

In searching out a mannerism for your character, it pays once again to return to the concept of stimulus/response. That's really another way of saying return to nature in making your CHOICES. What is the stimulus to which your mannerism is a response? Your character might squint quickly from time to time when he's nervous, if he happens to be a proof reader or have an occupation that taxes his eyes. If you're playing a hooker, you might lick your lips seductively in order to aid in pursuing your OBJECTIVE. Will you lick your lips because they're dry? Is licking your lips something you enjoy or is it something you know your 'johns' will respond to? Does licking your lips give you control over the john who succumbs to your ploy? Any and every mannerism you work with needs OR-GANIC depth for us to sense its TRUTH. Raise your eyebrows up and down quickly a few times and smile. Unmistakably Groucho.

Sometimes a mannerism is just a reflection of who *we* are and serves no purpose in playing a character. Some actors have nervous habits that are also mannerisms. They may drum their fingers on the table incessantly. If they're playing a jazz musician it could work, but if they are playing a psychiatrist taking control of an hysterical patient, it could confuse an audience.

It may seem like a mechanical way of creating, but if done properly, it isn't. The genesis of what you're feeling can be expressed in a myriad of ways, not only in the way you are used to. Just find a way to express what is happening in you as the character might.

Method, The
An acting process, based in nature, used to make an actor's performance truthful and believable.

The man behind the Method is Constantin STANISLAVSKI[1]. Webster's defines the Stanislavski Method as, "a technique in acting by which an actor strives to empathize with the CHARACTER he is portraying so as to affect a realistic interpretation." Yes. Well almost. If it were that simple then the Method couldn't and wouldn't apply to stylized pieces, Shakespeare, or musicals. And it does. If we change the word 'realistic' to 'truthful', Mr. Webster would be closer to the mark.

---

[1] Constantin Stanislavski (1863–1938) was born of wealthy parents in Russia under the name Constantin Sergeyevich Alexeyev. He changed his name to Stanislavski as a way of protecting his family name during his first theatrical experiences. The only member of his family connected with the theatre was his grandmother, Marie Varley, who was a French actress.

Stanislavski's work as an actor, producer, director, and teacher lead to revolutionary changes in theatre. Through experiments in 'psychotechnique' or ways of understanding the mind, spirit and nature he created a kind of 'holistic' approach to acting. Anyone acting today is drawing on techniques pioneered by Stanislavski if he is interested in doing believable work.

Stanislavski observed a certain few actors of his time perform with INSPIRATION, a depth of SOUL, an IMMEDIACY of TRUTH that made audiences *feel* what was happening on stage, not merely understand it. Stanislavski studied these actors and developed what was referred to as a 'system' of techniques and exercises that would give other actors a way of achieving inspiration in their work as well.

One of the most intriguing statements regarding Stanislavski's system is a statement by him in 1936, just two years before his death. In a talk to actors and producers at the Moscow Art Theatre, Stanislavski said, in part: "There is only one system–creative organic nature. There is no other system. And we must remember that this so-called system (let us not talk of a system, but of the nature of creative art) does not remain stationary. It changes every day."[1] This is a most appealing and freeing statement regarding the Method, the System or any conscious plan to study acting. Here is another about books on the system from the same source:

There are no subjects dealing with the art of the stage that can be stowed away in books and taught with the idea of turning out different categories of creative units A, B, C. Man himself, the whole of him, is the book of creative art. And the longer you give him the wrong kind of tuition at school, the less conscious does he become of the creative powers within him, and the more he will rely on textbooks and external circumstances to make a career for himself, forgetting what it was that first drew him to the studio and how great his love was of the career he had chosen for himself when he entered the studio.

The Method in theatrical circles today is a term associated with Lee Strasberg and the work at The Actors Studio.[2] It was extrapolated from the process created by

---

[1] David Magarshack, Stanislavski - on the Art of the Stage, 1950 from the preface to the second edition.

[2] The Actors Studio was founded in New York by actor, and director Elia Kazan, producer Cheryl Crawford, and actor, director and teacher Robert Lewis in 1947. Shortly after its inception Lee Strasberg became its Artistic Director. Members of the acting unit are legendary as are members of the playwright's/director's unit. Actors may audition for membership in the Studio with a five minute scene. If an actor is accepted he is accepted as a lifetime member at no cost to him.

Stanislavski. Actually, people writing about the changes in theatre in America during the 1930s through the 1950s referred to this way of working as a method. In time it became known as The Method. Great theatre artists such as Marlon Brando, Elia Kazan, Stella Adler, and others were said to be 'Method actors'. There are well over two hundred books, both in and out of print, dealing with Strasberg's Method and Stanislavski's system. Let's begin by looking at some common ideas of what the Method is and isn't.

"Be a tree!" was the most common cliché one heard about the method. The next most frequent comment was, "method actors just scratch their chests and mumble" (I think a critic was talking about Brando's performance as Stanley Kowalski in *Streetcar*...). The element of interest to most actors today is, "What can I do to insure that audiences will believe my acting?"

Throughout this book there is continuing reference to the NATURAL idea of stimulus/response. What might have been Stanislavski's stimulus for the response of a new system of acting? It might have been his OBSERVATION of some bad acting, or perhaps his observation of some wonderful acting that seemed all too rare amidst all the mediocre acting of the time.

Let's imagine what Stanislavski was dealing with in terms of theatre in the early 1900s. At that time there was a revolution going on in the theatre. Lighting!

In the centuries before the late 1800s, say from the Greeks through to Elizabethan theatre, the stage was first lit by the sun. Plays were performed in the afternoon and mostly out of doors. Shakespeare's Globe had no roof. The point is that the actors and the audience were equally lit. Then, roofs were built onto the theatres, and plays were performed in the evening. The theatre needed lighting. First maybe with rush candles, then gaslight, limelight, and then electric lights. Up until electricity, the house was still lighted during the play. Both audience and actor were equalized by light. The audience participated in the play because they could see and be seen by the actors. Members of the audience then wanted to see each other as much as the play.

In the 1880s with electricity, the stage became brighter than at any other time in the history of the theatre. Electricity is and was expensive, and it became too expensive to keep the house lights on. Now the audience was in darkness. Only the stage was illuminated. When actors first encountered electric lighting, the first thing they had to deal with was that they could no longer see the audience. Rather than play to the audience, which had been the custom, they turned to face each other. They began to talk to each other rather than *represent* talking to each other. That is also about the time when dramatists like Strindberg and Ibsen began writing naturalistic plays.

If you take some modern actors and put them in a candlelit theatre, then ask them to play a particular moment from a play, you and they will find that our modern acting techniques are not as effective. The audience can't see the actor feel the anger. It's too dark. The actor, in order to communicate anger to the audience has to resort to gestures such as clenching fists and moving arms up and down or other large movements that can be seen in a small amount of light and understood by the audience. In candlelight it's clear. Shine a light on it and it appears overacted, representational, and silly.

During the early 1900s there were actors who had an instinct about what would work on stage. Stanislavski noticed that natural acting worked better, and that a few actors seemed to be able to do it naturally.

That is when Stanislavski put together a plan to find a way to act according to the laws of nature, as opposed to what might appear to work theatrically.

Stanislavski looked at psychological MOTIVATIONS for ACTIONS. He looked at real emotions, and borrowed the stimulus/response concept from nature. Making CHOICES based in nature is the cornerstone of the system. If the CHARACTER gets angry, as an actor you don't *try* and get angry. You create a real stimulus for your own personal anger. In other words, if you want to create an effect, you must first create the cause. In real life we don't want to experience the PAIN of grieving for the loss of a loved one. We want to avoid the feeling. We want to distance ourselves from it. Yet when faced with the TASK of creating grief, many actors think about what makes them sad instead of creating a reality (SENSE MEMORY) and choosing an ACTION to pursue.

Lee Strasberg interpreted the system for American actors in the 1930s with the Group Theatre and later at the Actors Studio. Strasberg called it, the Method. He formulated many acting exercises to train actors to get in touch with and express their emotions. He focused primarily on the use of personal emotional choices. There was and still is much controversy over this aspect of the Method. Many feel that it was exploitive and irresponsible. There was the famous schism between the approach to the method taught by Stella Adler and that of the Strasberg school; Adler focusing more on the use of IMAGINATION, ACTION and GIVEN CIRCUMSTANCES rather than 'digging up emotional pain from the past'.

There will always be disagreements over how art should be created and even whether or not a particular piece is art. A cohesive approach to art is a way of using techniques to accomplish your artistic goals and clearly express your natural talent. The collection and mastery of those techniques is called CRAFT. You can't be an effective artist until the craft is absorbed. The craft has to 'click in' spontaneously to be of value.

There are many actors who eschew the Method. They are method actors anyway. Why? Going back to Stanislavski, every actor wants to be believable to the audience, to his fellow actors and to himself. Every actor strives to appear TRUTHFUL. Every actor has his own way of creating truth. Some are effective, some are not, some are ordinary and some are brilliant, whatever the method.

Mise-en-scène
The overall look and feel of a scene or production. Pronounced MEEZ-AHN-SEN.

When one speaks of the mise-en-scène of the play, one means the look and feel of the production. The staging of the actors, the set, lighting, costumes, sound effects, and music all create an environment, a mood, a feeling that helps tell the story the way the director envisions it.

When you are being paid above scale for your acting and directing, you will find yourself using phrases like mise-en-scène.

Moment to moment
A description of the result of the Method, when employed correctly. The creative goal in committing to the process. Living in the present from one section to the next.

The phrase 'moment to moment' is a METHOD acting cliché. Like any cliché it is used often because it is based on a sound TRUTH. Moment to moment is what it feels like and looks like to deal with each moment as it comes without ANTICIPATING.

If you're working correctly, if you believe your surroundings, pursue your OBJECTIVE with personal ACTIONS, then you can enjoy a certain RELAXATION or lack of tension. As you do what you need to and deal with any OBSTACLES that arise as they arise, you are described as being in the moment. As this happens successively in the scene and the play, you are moving from one moment to the next moment. Moment to moment.

Monologue
A section of the play spoken by one actor as either part of a scene or alone on stage. See also SOLILOQUY.

There are very few true monologues. Most text that we call monologues are really sections of scenes in which one CHARACTER has the larger part of the dialogue.

Actors face monologues in two main situations. When they arise within the context of the play and when they are removed from the play to be used for AUDITIONS. Each is to be approached differently.

When a monologue comes up in the middle of the play, you have the whole play to tell the audience who your character is. You have your OBJECTIVE and ACTION built in. The momentum of the play is there to help you. If the monologue takes place within a scene, then you know your PRIOR CIRCUMSTANCES: to whom you're talking and what it is you want and need to say and do.

Here's a trick, look at the last two lines of the monologue. Whatever is contained in the last two lines is the reason you opened your mouth to say the first two lines. Make CHOICES that JUSTIFY what and why you say what you say before you reach the last two lines.

Beware of the 'memory monologue'. When the subject of the monologue takes the character into the past, be careful it doesn't take you into an 'acting the past' type behavior. You've seen actors do monologues from the character's past. They stare up at the lights to INDICATE that they're remembering something wonderful, painful, wistful, or sensual. The problem is their action becomes 'to remember' or worse to 'try to remember'. Instead use the memory in the text as a stimulus to do something in the present. The action of the scene after all takes place in the present. Make a choice that uses something your character did, saw, or experienced to do something brand new now.

Aside from plays, monologues plague actors more acutely when used for auditions. Do one or two two-minute monologues. Do two contrasting pieces, one classical and one contemporary. These are familiar instructions to all actors.

One of the problems with monologues for use in auditions is that they don't allow for 'give and take' between an actor and another character as a scene would. The actor must create both parts. How can he or she really be surprised by what the other character is going to do, when he's creating and playing both roles? Regardless, monologues are a part of our theatrical life. We must find a way to deal with them, accept them, and actually enjoy them.

The first questions to ask in PREPARING an audition monologue are, "To whom am I talking? A character who is or isn't there, to myself, the audience, or the auditioners?"[1] Once you answer those questions, you can make some choices.

If you're talking to another character who doesn't happen to be there, you've got to create the other person so SPECIFICALLY that you actually respond to him. Instead of trying to imagine the other character, you can create the other character using SENSE MEMORY. You can sensorily create people from your own life and make choices pertaining to them.

If you're talking to yourself, you are most probably in a contemporary play. Remember the saying, people who talk to themselves are either crazy or they have money in the bank? Think about when you actually do talk to yourself. Find a real reason why you might need to express yourself by talking to yourself.

If however you're working on a monologue independent of a play, for class or an audition, then you must

---

[1] In a professional audition situation your best strategy is simply to ask the auditioner(s) whether to use them or not. Some will ask you to play to them while others will ask you to play to an empty chair. All will usually thank you for asking. Be prepared to play it either way.

work harder to find a strong action in order to pursue your objective. Also, if you're working on an audition, you might have your own personal objective that has less to do with the play and more to do with showing different sides of *you*, playing various levels of emotion and basically, trying to get the job. These objectives may have nothing to do with the play. This happens because you're not selling the play you're selling yourself, your talent, and ability. Here are some factors to consider.

In an audition for Chekhov's *The Seagull*, an actor introduced it by saying he wanted to show his original interpretation of the work. Whether or not the director agrees with his interpretation is immaterial. Under these circumstances we can see the actor's courage and inventiveness. We can accept almost anything he does because the ground rules he sets tell us he is intentionally trying something different. This can be very effective provided he's a good actor.

I remember an actress auditioning with a monologue from a short story. That's a wonderful idea given the story has action not just narrative. This actor chose *Uncle Wiggley in Connecticut* by J. D. Salinger. As I was familiar with the story, I asked her whether or not she worked on being drunk, which was part of the character's GIVEN CIRCUMSTANCES. Being drunk allowed her to say things she may never have said otherwise. The actress said she chose not to work on drunk. An odd choice in this instance.

If the director isn't familiar with the piece, he or she might be impressed. If, however, the director does know the piece, then the choice of not dealing with an important element of the story shows the director how she makes choices.

In class you can always improve a monologue just by going back to basics. Generally we will see a monologue and ask the actor what it is he has worked on to create the behavior we just witnessed. Although sometimes we ADJUST the choice, most of the time we help the actor to be more specific and sharpen his focus. Here is what happens.

After we see the monologue performed once, the actor is asked two questions. To whom are you talking and what do you want to do? Assuming those choices will be effective, the actor will be asked to use SENSE

MEMORY to create a person from his own life who makes him feel the way the character in the play does.

The actor is then asked to place his hands on the person's face or shoulders and feel the skin and bone structure to get a sense of the temperature and texture. He will create and see the person's eyes, touch the hair, etc. When, in the actor's eyes we see that the person is really there for him, he is directed to do an IMAGINARY MONOLOGUE. Using his own words, the actor tells the person something he might never say if the person were really there. When the actor clicks into the action and becomes fully INVOLVED, he might be asked to continue the exercise using random numbers or GIBBERISH. Now he rehearses only the behavior. Once grounded in the immediate behavior, he continues talking to the person he's created, but now he might drop the numbers and go directly to the text. He's cautioned not to make any intellectual sense of the text. He's just to use the words as if they were the random numbers. This exercise commits the actor fully. The class has a better understanding of the monologue and the actor learns to strive continually to rehearse behavior, not just intellectual choices.

This behavioral approach, it must be emphasized, is balanced with good old-fashioned EXTERNAL WORK on the TEXT ANALYSIS and TEXT TECHNIQUE. Think of it this way. The INTERNAL behavioral choices we make, that make us feel and get our motor going, are like a powerful locomotive. All of the external text work is like laying down the train tracks. One is not effective without the other. Separately each stands for tremendous potential. Put them together and they will take you great distances in record time.

Motivation
The reason for your action.

In order to convict someone of a crime in a court of law, one of the mandatory factors is a motive. Without it there is no case. The jury will not believe you. To act and to be believed you need a motive. Actors want to be believed therefore actors must be concerned with the motivation for the ACTIONS they take.

You begin with an action, say 'to charm'. Then you JUSTIFY your action. "If I charm her, she'll talk to me." Now you need a MOTIVATION. "I'd like to ask her to dinner."

If you look up motivation in the index of the many books on acting it may surprise you that most of the books don't mention it at all. The term has fallen from favor. Nevertheless, the idea is important. Using the above example you can see how a personal choice, like wanting a date, can lead to truthful behavior.

When you have a real reason, when you're motivated, your role will be easier to play. The audience will also find it easier to participate in the action.

If you don't like the word 'motivation' because of some cliché image of an old fashioned method actor, just have a really good, personal reason to do what you do. Create the cause and discover the effect.

Mugging
Broad facial gestures designed to entertain the audience at the expense of genuinely playing your part.

Mugging is INDICATING to the ninth power. It is demonstrating with your face what you're feeling or what you're supposed to be doing to the other CHARACTER. Let's say you see a beautiful woman and you don't trust the audience or yourself to let them know you think she's a knockout. You might be tempted to raise your eyebrows up and down several times a la Groucho Marx.[1] That is mugging: relying on superficial acting and using your 'mug' to do it. If you think about it, why limit your expression to just your face? You have your whole body, your mind and your SOUL with which to express yourself.

In a sense, mugging becomes a substitute for really doing your work. If that happens, it's the audience who gets mugged.

---

[1] Actually it isn't mugging when Marx does it. Groucho Marx was using a gesture that became his trade mark. It was a deliberate choice used to communicate a truth to the audience.

Natural (on acting)

A brief discussion of the differences between truthful, real, authentic, and natural acting.

> They're gonna put me in the movies,
> They're gonna make a big star out o' me.
> Gonna make a film about a man who's sad and
>   lonely,
> And all I gotta do is act *NATURALLY*.[1]

Every actor, at first glance, wants to be natural because it implies being believed. There are actors who attain a natural quality in their work yet their work is not thorough enough to allow them to be believed. It's as if being 'natural' gets confused with being 'casual'. In the literal sense of the word, 'acting natural' would be to make CHOICES based on nature as opposed to what the actor thinks might look good theatrically. Natural acting is not the same as TRUTHFUL acting.

Natural acting is a result. It's a description of your work given by other people who watch you. It is not a particular school of acting.

Some actors strive to be real, but reality may not contain theatrical truth either. Theatrical truth exists within the GIVEN CIRCUMSTANCES of the play. When a friend directed a production of John Steinbeck's *Of Mice and Men*, he asked the prop department to design a 'dead puppy' for the scene in which Lenny inadvertently squeezes his pet puppy too tight and kills it. The prop pup looked so real that the audience withdrew from the story of the play and became concerned for the well-being of what it thought was a real animal. The next night, props substituted a rolled-up pair of black socks. The new unrealistic prop allowed the audience to stay with the theatrical metaphor, the truth of the play.

---

[1] "Act Naturally", John Russell and Vonie Morrison, Bakersfield, CA: Blue Book Music, BMI, 1963–1971.

Authenticity occurs when an actor fully immerses himself in what he wants, and what he wants to do to get it. There is a CONCENTRATION of focus that releases an ENERGY, or stage presence. The behavior is genuine, it contains truth. The result of that process will appear natural.

Notes
Adjustments and/or critique given by the director.

You've just finished a long and difficult REHEARSAL. You're trying to get a line on the CHARACTER and incorporate what you've learned from the playwright and the director. You've spent hours EXPLORING and struggling. Now you want to go out with the cast for a cup of coffee or a drink, or just go home. No! The director calls, "Notes!"

Notes are simply the director trying to bring the play together. The notes are sometimes just technical. "Notice the room for a moment before you start to speak," the director might say. Or, "Never put your hands in your pockets in this scene. In the whole play!" Or, my all time favorite, "The opening is dragging guys, pick up the PACE." (See TEMPO) In any case, notes should be very helpful.

First employ the notes. Write the notes down in your script in pencil and go over them until they're part of the play. Your director not only has a concept of what he wants the play to look like, but also a third eye that can tell you how you're coming off in the play.

If you're not sure of your director's note, develop the habit of repeating the note back to the director. This allows the director to know that she has been heard and understood. It eliminates miscommunication. This is particularly valuable in on-camera work where time is incredibly expensive, especially if it's your first time working with the director. Some directors become so tense under the pressures of production that they may not tolerate your repeating their notes back to them. Judge for yourself.

Here is some advice to players whose directors give them rotten notes. Listen carefully to the director and never argue. You won't win. Instead say this, "Thank you very much, that's very helpful—I'm having a problem though. I wonder if you can help me?" All directors love to be asked for help. "You see if I enter STAGE RIGHT, I'm afraid I might be pulling focus from Hamlet during the most important part of the play, how can I minimize that?" In all likelihood, the director will leave you alone throughout the rest of the production and focus attention on the guy who isn't off book yet.

Sometimes new actors, in a sincere desire to help, will offer their notes to you. "I think the scene will be better if you would only come in on cue after I say my line." Or, "Act like you like me when I blow my nose." New actors may need to be reminded that there's only one director. Depending on your relationship with the actor giving you notes, you may want to make your director aware of 'alternative suggestions'. Or you may want to say, "Bug off!"

Objective
What the character wants.

There must always be a reason for an actor to come on stage. An actor is playing a CHARACTER who wants something from someone else or from a situation. What he wants to accomplish is his OBJECTIVE.

There will often be more than one objective for a character throughout a play or a scene. There is also the overall, main objective to which the smaller objectives lead. (SUPER-OBJECTIVE).

The term objective is often used interchangeably with ACTION and INTENTION by teachers and directors. There are important differences that should be discussed so you can both understand and apply the concept behind the label.

As stated above, an objective is what the character wants. In order for you to make a CHOICE that will give your character depth, it's a good idea to keep asking "why" after each answer you come up with as to what the objective is.

For example, if your objective is to ask for a date from the prettiest, most popular girl in the school, ask why? Is it because you need to make an impression, or because you have an image of yourself that won't allow you to be seen with anybody else. Or could it be that she just happens to be the love of your life and you need this date to prove it to her.

As you answer these questions, you're really engaging in a process of delving deeper into the character's real needs or wants. The character will emerge as fuller and you will choose stronger actions in order to pursue your objective.

Objects
Physical items pertaining to your character and your surroundings. In sense memory, it's the thing you choose to work on..

In the SENSE MEMORY exercises, actors EXPLORE objects. It will usually begin with your MORNING DRINK and move on to the MIRROR, for shaving or putting on make-up. Or it could be a PERSONAL OBJECT, something that has an emotional connection for you, which you can sense memorize.

When you first learn sensory work, you don't refer to your breakfast drink as coffee, tea, or milk, but rather as the 'object'. In this way you avoid drawing conclusions about what your intellect and head memory tell you about what you 'think' the item really is. If you use your house keys as an object and you think about them, you're apt to say, "Yeah, so what. They're house keys. I know all about 'em. What about it?" You think you know all about your keys because you deal with them every day. You're right. In a sensory exercise, though, you need to skip that part about what you know and adopt a mind-set that wants to know more. You need to come from curiosity, from wonder. By calling your keys an object, you allow for questions about the object. Weight, smell, size, function—all become questions to explore if you can proceed AS IF you don't know the answers.

Objects you surround yourself with will stimulate your inner and outer life depending of course on what they are. When a set designer or an art director adds an item or prop to the set, there's a reason. As an actor, find the reason and PERSONALIZE it so that it affects both you and your audience.

Observation
The detailed study of nature and reality for incorporation into your art.

When you pay close attention to seemingly simple every-day occurrences, you often find there are small things happening that you've never considered or thought about before. By adding these bits of 'insignifica' to your work, you become more specific and at the same time more believable.

If you are playing a surgeon, you could rely on your idea of what a surgeon is, of what you think he or she does. Or you can find a hospital and try to watch what it is that surgeons actually do. You can learn how they speak about their work to their colleagues, to their patients, to their families? Do all doctors behave in the same way? What are the differences in the doctors you observe?

You find the answers to these questions by observing the real life counterpart to the CHARACTER you are playing. Just by observing you can see small actions that in and of themselves you may not understand. But put them all together and they add up to a logic that creates a picture and a deeper understanding of the character, because you now know what the character does. And as the character you can do those things or get a sense of doing those things too.

In an old class exercise, we used to visit night court just to observe the characters and their behavior. We observed derelicts, prostitutes, attorneys, judges, police officers, even other spectators. We would study different MANNERISMS and were always aware of cause and effect. What made the accused approach the judge more slowly than usual? What caused the judge to sigh? What made the lawyer hesitate before speaking, and why was he dressed shabbily? We would choose a SPECIFIC character and recreate that individual in the studio devising different IMPROVISATIONAL scenarios to challenge us in our work.

Try this. If you're away from home, think about one small area of where you live. Maybe it's the living room with bookshelves. Remember just one shelf, its contents and the surrounding wall. How much detail can you recall. What books are there? What are their ages? Is there dust on some or all of the books? What colors and shapes do you see? When you're back at home, check out the shelf to see how accurate your recall was.

When your job is to create a character, a time period, or a living reality, rather than simply trying to represent it from your assumed speculation, try and observe as much as you can of the reality. Your research is a vital part of your HOMEWORK and your PREPARATION.

Obstacles
The barriers that prevent you from doing what you want to do.

Obstacles build CHARACTER, both in acting and in life. If your character's OBJECTIVE is to get money, revenge, fame, or love, and you get it right away, you have no conflict, and there is no challenge. There is no drama. There is a strong likelihood that it won't be theatrical either!

STANISLAVSKI advised actors to find the obstacles. The more insurmountable the obstacle appears, the harder you must work, the more committed you must be, and the more focus you must have.

What are the obstacles preventing you from getting what you or your character wants? You are on your way to an important job interview. You have prepared for weeks. You have been stricken with laryngitis but you cannot change your appointment because the person you're seeing will be out of town for two months. What do you do? Do you explain your condition to your potential employer and whisper your plans, or do you write your questions and answers on a pad of paper and show them to him? Or will you cancel the meeting?

What happens will depend on how strong your need is, how much you believe the situation, and how much risk you're willing to take. By finding the obstacle you strengthen your character's objective and your action.

Obstacles are opportunities. There is a saying, "We are continually faced by great opportunities brilliantly disguised as insoluble problems."

Opposites
Deepening your character by examining his or her other side.

When you think of the phrase 'two sides of the same coin', you're dealing with opposite views of the same OB-JECT. Heads is clearly different from tails, especially in a coin toss. But they are both a part of each other. Another popular phrase is 'The opposite of love is not hate, it's indifference'. Freud said that love and hate were interwoven. Yet on the surface they seem to be opposites.

Things are generally more complicated than they seem. No one is all good or all bad. Finding the obvious CHOICE is the first step. EXPLORING opposites is the continuation of the process of giving the CHARACTER depth and complexity.

A wonderful actor friend once shared his AUDITION strategy. He said, "I look at the obvious choice, then I give 'em 180 degrees the opposite. I know what most of the other actors are going to do; I'll be damned if I'm going to do that." It doesn't always work, of course, but it works frequently enough, and it gives him an edge both personally and theatrically.

Imagine that the TASK is to play a villain. There is usually an immediate rush to judgment that serves to proclaim our personal outrage at the actions this villain takes. Some actors, faced with the task of playing Hitler, will find a way subconsciously to let the audience know that they are acting. They need you to know that they are not really like that. They're just playing a part. Even though consciously they want to be a realistic, believable Hitler.

Suppose you investigated Hitler when he was charming. What made him laugh? What made him love? Some people will be upset at the very thought of these questions. Others will approach the problem more objectively. In one sense, the more questions you pose the more stimuli you create for yourself and for the character. It's when we or the character deal with many different things that we learn the most about whom we're playing. It's easier to understand something when we look at it as a whole and not just at one side. We and the characters we play are the sum total of our differences. We can't really appreciate a great play without knowing a bad play. You can't have day without night, hot without cold, plus without minus.

In *My Life in Art*[1], STANISLAVSKI says;

> ...you are painting the picture in only one
> color, and black only becomes black when
> some white is introduced for the sake of con-
> trast. So let just a bit of white color as well as
> some other colors of the rainbow into your
> role. There will be contrast, variety and
> truth....When you play a good man look for the
> places where he is evil, and in an evil man look
> for the places where he is good.

In working with opposites, you will actually create
more possibilities to solving the problem of the character. Try playing with opposites in your next REHEARSAL.

Organic
*A description of a performance where the origin and progres-
sion of truthful behavior is evident.*

Within the school of METHOD acting, one hears the word
organic thrown around frequently. When you say this
word to a new actor, he usually doesn't understand quite
what you mean.

Webster says organic means, 'having the characteristics of an organism : developing in the manner of a living plant or animal.' We've all seen acting that did not
have the characteristics of an organism, human or otherwise. Even if the audience does believe the actor and the
resultant behavior, that is not enough.

We not only need to believe the actor, we need to
believe the behavior in context with the scene and the
story. We need to sense a natural development of ACTION.

One reason method actors use the term 'organic' is
that it is brought up continuously in the writings of
STANISLAVSKI who sought to create a theatre that was vital.
He wanted to have actors 'live the part'. By that he
meant the actor MOTIVATED, taking the same actions as the
CHARACTER. He doesn't imitate what the character does, he
finds a real and personal JUSTIFICATION to really do what the
playwright says he does. It is when the actor takes on the

---

[1]*My Life in Art* Constantin Stanislavski (Boston: Little, Brown,
and Company, 1924) Reprinted in 1991 by Routledge/Theatre
Arts Books, New York

real PASSION of the character and it overlaps, so to speak, with his own, that a living breathing character, one with depth, emerges in what appears to be a life of his own. He appears to be playing his part each time as if for the first time. True creativity occurs through nature. Therefore if the theatre artist is to create truly he must adopt the principles of creative, organic nature.

Over the Top (O.T.T.)

Primarily a British term for playing the largest choice possible and making a full commitment.

The idea of acting over the top seems like the OPPOSITE approach to THE METHOD. In the Method you work from the inside out, that is you create a MOTIVATION and react. When you go over the top, you start with the desired result, then work out how to get it. This is an EXTERNAL, not an INTERNAL technique.

Sometimes actors will REHEARSE a scene and wait for a feeling to happen. There is a reluctance to express large behavior. If your CHARACTER is angry, take a risk and really go over the top in expressing it.

Staying NATURAL is a great way to hide mediocre acting. The acting really isn't good, but the performance is so small it is not readily noticeable. Playing it big isn't what's bad. It's the bigness that shows up the bad acting, if it's there in the first place.

Try it by doing your piece out loud. You can't go over the top by doing it in your head. Take your MONOLOGUE or scene and break it down into smaller sections, sentences, or even phrases. This has nothing to do with BEATS. Do the first section and take it over the top. If it should be loud, shout it as loud as you can. If you think it's soft, make it very soft. If it's slow, make it e x t r a o r d i n a r i l y s l o w w w. If it's fast, say it vry fst. In other words, regardless of how you actually feel, exaggerate the hell out of it. Now with the next phrase, find the GEAR CHANGE and do the same thing. Don't be concerned with what's real or even truthful at this stage. This is not the result, it is simply a means to a possible end.

Let's be absolutely clear. To exaggerate doesn't mean you should act badly. If your CHOICE is one that makes you upset, then to exaggerate it would be to increase the size of your choice, say to a choice that makes you furious.

Watching this done in a class of some fifteen actors, you see the first couple of actors fail miserably at it. As we progress through the line of actors, you can hear actors say, "I know what he means, why doesn't she just really go for it?" Yet when they get up there, they usually fare no better. It isn't easy. The results of this exercise, when performed full out, are stunning. To do it takes courage. Courage to risk looking really silly. Take the chance! If you risk the slap, you might get a kiss. The exercise is a blueprint for risk taking.

EXERCISE

Tell someone you love her. Go over the top.
When you say it, mean it.

Overacting

Acting more than is necessary. Artificial acting. Pushing.

Overacting is usually the result of poor PREPARATION, poor training, lack of talent or understanding. Sometimes it is done to cover insecurity.

If you don't think you are enough, you will over compensate by doing more, too much. You will push what isn't really there. You will be overacting.

If you spend most of your time thinking about the CHARACTER and behaving as the character you will invoke your subconscious to be in harmony with your external stage craft techniques. Your actor's ACTIONS will INSTINC-TIVELY and naturally overlap the actions of the character. You will have a reason to observe your partner for signs that you are succeeding in accomplishing your OBJECTIVE.

If, however, you neglect your HOMEWORK and your preparation, you will resort to stage tricks, CLICHÉS, and imitation. Your work will be described by your audience and certainly your fellow cast members as overacting. As Hamlet said to the player, "Pray you avoid it."

Pace
Picking up cues in order to affect timing.

"Pick up the pace!" It's the battle cry of many a director. It can also mean, "I didn't direct this as well as I would have liked and it drags like hell. Since we don't have any more time, just do it faster."

Every script has timing built into it. It comes from the RHYTHM of the CHARACTERS, which in turn comes from the rhythm of the playwright. This is what should establish pace.

Often in the third or fourth week of REHEARSAL, we lose a sense of pace. This is usually because the actors are still incorporating BLOCKING and STAGE BUSINESS. One solution is to have a sit-down LINE REHEARSAL. Magically, the pace is picked up.

Pain (non-sensory)
Personal emotional discomfort arising from emotional exploration of your part.

In acting there is much talk of reexperiencing pain, dredging up the painful past to create emotional pain—real pain.

Most of us want to avoid pain like the plague. Every so often, in an actor's work, either in class or in a professional job, he will contact real, personal, emotional pain. As soon as that happens fear takes over and tension seizes the muscles. Creativity retreats. Next time it happens consider this:

Most of the time, when emotional pain occurs in real life we never asked for it. We try to disown it, get rid of it, get past it. It is real life pain that comes from outside us. It enters us through no choice of our own.

When we are practicing our CRAFT, we may contact pain that is already within ourselves. Pain that has been covered up for years. This pain is being touched on by CHOICE. The difference is this pain was already impressed on us in the past. We artists have the wonderful opportunity to take the real pain already in us and express it outwardly. We can sublimate a pain we judge to be awful. We can make it sublime by sending it outwards to be part of a total creation.

If you have not had this experience before, then the first time you reexperience your real pain in a class or REHEARSAL, you will be conditioned to respond as if it were real. You may get tense, scared. You may try to hold it back. It *was* real. Now it's recurring because you chose it. RELAX. Breathe. Express the pain through the playwright's words. Now you can sublimate what was genuinely negative into what is now artistically positive. This is one of the great things about theatre.

Particularization
The process of making your choice specific.

"Okay, particularize it!" is a command that used to be given by thousands of acting teachers years ago, more than it seems to be used today. Of course it depends on your teacher. It's one of those 'jargonny' words that seem to exist to intimidate the person who doesn't know what it means. It is one of the reasons for this book.

Particularize, as it is defined above, means to be SPECIFIC in whatever CHOICE you make.

There is a scene in the movie *Body Double* that shows an acting student being brutalized emotionally by his omnipotent teacher. The teacher shouts, "Particularize that!" while the student is going through an emotional breakdown.

Perhaps years ago a teacher who was earnestly trying to get an actor to become specific, told the actor to be particular in choosing his OBJECT. In repeating the concept (seventy-five percent of teaching is repetition), he began to say, "Now make the object particular." In reminding this and each successive actor who wasn't yet making specific choices, the teacher found a kind of shorthand in the language. He made 'particular' into a verb. 'Specificallize' doesn't sound as good as 'particularize'. Those who were impressed began to copy the new word and a term was born.

Sometimes it seems that if we teachers didn't make up ten-dollar words, we might, God forbid, be on the same level as our plebeian students. Well, we're all in the same boat. We all share fears, desires, and triumphs. This business is tough enough. We must all help each other. So to repeat: to particularize is to make particular. Just be specific. It will affect you far more than a general choice. And it simply makes good sense.

Passion
The power behind the art. The pure individual driving force. The lifeblood of the soul.

This is not an acting term. It's a way of life. It is the most necessary component to act and to live—well.

The word 'passion', according to Webster's, comes from Middle English and Old French. It means suffering, being acted upon.

All the technique and mastery of CRAFT in the world won't help if you aren't in touch with your passion. Passion is your abiding attention and CONCENTRATION on a thing or an idea. It is a force that heats up your body, quickens your breathing and brings your SOUL to the surface of life.

When we witness an actor expressing his or her passion we participate in the performance because our own passions are aroused. When we seize the opportunity to express our own passions, theatrically or otherwise, there is no other feeling in the world quite like it. It embraces both serenity and orgasm as the protons and electrons of universal atoms of pure creativity.

In our classes at Drama Project, we do 'passion workouts'. These are exercises to encourage the theatrical expression of passion.

An actor gets up in front of the class and begins by telling us something personal about which he feels passionate. It can be a philosophy, an idea, a hobby, or even a sweater seen in a store window and coveted. It can be anything as long as one feels passionate about it. The actor addresses us as if he was a Sunday morning television evangelist. He is encouraged to go OVER THE TOP in his expression, even if it is 'pushed' at first. When he hits a high point in the 'sermon', he sharply points his finger to the sky and we all join in with a resounding "YEAH!!!" or "AMEN!!!", whichever he chooses.

One good actor who was very shy stood out. She was a small, dark-haired woman in her forties. She claimed she had nothing to talk about. She couldn't think of a thing to be passionate about. Then she announced that she had something in her mind, but she didn't know if it would be alright. She said it was something that she cared deeply about though. She began the exercise. All of a sudden her thoughts transformed her. She straightened her body and lifted her chin. In a strong, powerful voice she said, "My friends, I'm here to tell you about MONEY!" "Money is the thing that will give you all of your dreams! Money can give you the power to do anything you want! You may be ashamed to admit it, but you know how much you want MONEY! Don't you?" "YEAH!!!" shouted the class. It didn't matter what her subject was. Many of the people who cheered their support didn't agree with her message. But we all identified with her passion. And we all felt her passion trigger our own.

In the weeks and months after the initial exercise is done a few times, the actors repeat the exercise, only this time with out going over the top. Just no more or less than they feel at the moment. The passion is now expressed calmly but still fervently. There is a deep sense of substance. It isn't long before we recognize the actors' passions in their next SCENE or MONOLOGUE.

Try the exercise yourself. Do it alone in front of a mirror, with a theatre group, or a group of trusted friends. We all feel passion. Some of us benefit from a structured technique that allows us to REHEARSE the expression of it.

Patterning

A limiting byproduct of rehearsal, where the words in the text have the same timing and inflection no matter what the choice.

When actors make CHOICES that are intellectual rather than resulting from a process,[1] patterning occurs.

When you make different choices, yet the lines still come out with the same stresses and intonations in the exact same way, you're stuck in a pattern.

---

[1] Process, in acting terminology, means creating the cause that leads to the result. If the result is anger, create the source of the SPECIFIC anger. If the result is exhilaration, find the specific thing that personally exhilarates you in terms of the CHARACTER.

Patterning is the manifestation of habits. Habits in and of themselves are neither good nor bad. Habits inhibit the flow of IMPULSES. They impede spontaneity. They postpone creativity. If creativity implies something happening for the first time, habits are the opposite. Habits are behaviors performed on a regular basis without much thought.

Go back to your choice of a stimulus and express it nonverbally, take a vacation from the words. After your PREPARATION, express no more or less than what you're feeling using random numbers or GIBBERISH instead of the TEXT. Yes, it sounds weird but it helps to cure patterning. It will key you into what's really happening within you, in the MOMENT. Now go back to the text and say the words, aloud as if they were the numbers. If your behavior is genuine, but you're not telling the story of the play, don't change your process—change your choice.

EXERCISE

Begin shaving on a different side of your face from usual.

Begin applying your makeup in a different order.

Pause

A momentary stopping of either dialogue, movement or both, serving to continue dramatic action, not impede it.

A pause means you stop, right? _ _ _ _ _ _ _ _ _ _ _ _ _ _ _
Wrong! You might not say your next line for a moment, you may even freeze briefly, but you're not doin' nothin'. I've intentionally employed the double negative because, as my old English teacher used to say, "If you ain't got none, you must have some."

Pauses can be wonderfully effective when a director adds them to scenes. Pauses can create dramatic tension, they can also be used for emphasis and mood. Pauses are written in scripts by playwrights, suggested by acting teachers, demanded by directors, and experimented with by actors.

Pauses are a way of furthering dramatic ACTION. If the play or your director asks you to pause, you hold for a BEAT. You don't come to a dead stop. Unless your stopping in some way makes the action move better. A pause is simply a nonverbal way of perpetuating the action.

One of the great comedy moments of yesteryear was in a sketch with Jack Benny. Benny, (who always played the cheap skate) was being held up at gunpoint. "Your money or your life!" commanded the robber. This was followed by silence. A long pause. After which Benny replied, "I'm thinking it over." If you ask people who remember the bit, they will say that he paused but they won't say that he wasn't doin' nothin'.

Personalization
To endow an object or another person in a scene with something or someone personal to you.

Personalization is the act of making an element of the scene that in actuality carries little or no meaning for you into something personal. It is a part of SUBSTITUTION. You are substituting something personal for something in the play that isn't.

If you make CHOICES that are based on your intellectual understanding of the play, then, at best, the audience will understand what you're doing and what you're about. If, however, you make choices that are personal to you, you will INVOLVE your whole self in your CHARACTER. Audience members will not only understand, they will feel with you too.

Personalization is a term one doesn't hear much any more. Many directors and teachers simply deal with the underlying concept of making story elements of the play personal to the actors rather than use the term 'personalize'.

Physical Action
The physical manifestation of your action.

The term PHYSICAL ACTION was first used by STANISLAVSKI to describe an ACTION that could be physically accomplished. It was the latest development in Stanislavski's system.

In 1935 Stanislavski began to use what he called the Method of Physical Actions as an alternative to the earlier variations of his 'system'. Rather than spending time in lengthy analytical REHEARSALS,[1] exploring AFFECTIVE MEMORY, Stanislavski began to rely directorially on physical actions as an outgrowth of the GIVEN CIRCUMSTANCES. In one sense, it was the formal or long term for action. Any CHOICE of action needs to be SPECIFIC. It also needs to be contained within what Stanislavski referred to as 'through-action', or the chain of actions from the beginning to the end of the play that serves the CHARACTER'S needs.

Once you decide 'to charm' your partner, for example, you then will pursue a physical action , a physical manifestation of what you want to do. You might for instance pull her chair out for her when sitting at the table. You might fix his tie before he goes to work. These are small, effective physicalizations of your actions. Larger choices would be to slap or kiss your partner depending on the circumstances. More important than the physical action is the truth contained in it, stemming from the logic of the scene.

Many teachers and directors today use the term 'physical action' to mean the actual physical activities, or stage business, that the actor does. Which one is correct is not the issue. The labels are not important; the concept is. It is important to know what your director or teacher means and what she wants.

The director's primary job is to make the play clear to the audience. One usually begins by literally staging the physical actions first. Scene: a woman is being amorously pursued by a man. She says, "I don't want to be in this position!" She is referring to her emotional position, but the lines allow for physicalizing the scene so that she is actually under him as he tries to make love to her. In another scene the husband receives news of his wife's infidelity. He physicalizes wanting to kill her by throwing her picture against the wall. The physical actions serve to clarify the scene for both the actors and the audience.

Preparation

What you do prior to performance to influence your behavior and create your character to its fullest. Focusing your attention on details that propel you into the scene.

---

[1] Stanislavsky had 157 rehearsals for the Moscow Art Theatre's 1930 production of *Othello*. Despite exhaustive preparation, *Othello* was critically unsuccessful. It closed after ten performances.

In any professional craft there is preparation. There are things you need to do *before* you do the things you need to do. A painter stretches his canvas and lays out his palette. A surgeon studies X-rays, scrubs, and lays out instruments before the operation. *An Actor Prepares* is the title STANISLAVSKI, gave to his first book. Preparation is what you do before you perform to make your performance happen.

You are moving from the circumstances in your real life to the GIVEN CIRCUMSTANCES in the play. You need to focus your attention on some element, some cause or stimulus existing in the play. It could be something that involves the PRIOR CIRCUMSTANCES in the scene you're playing. For example, if I must enter the scene to confront my partner regarding an injustice he has done to me, I must create a CHOICE for the cause of my trouble. It will be something I can focus on quickly that will change the way I feel and stimulate behavior that is appropriate for the scene. A SENSE MEMORY choice is perfect for this. If you need to come in DRUNK, find a choice to stimulate that behavior, or the illusion of drunk behavior. You could use a sweet SMELL, an intoxicating cologne, that when sniffed for an extended period of time creates in you a drunk-like sensation. Or you might try SUNSHINE at the beach, if it makes you drowsy and looks to others as if you're drunk.

Your choice should also be linked to your PHYSICAL ACTION. If you're coming in drunk what will you actually do? Sit down? Fall down? If you're entering elated, you might embrace someone or do a zany dance.

Did you ever wonder what it might have been like before all of these acting techniques were touted as 'vital to good acting'? Take a look at some of the greats from the past. Names like Tommaso Salvini, Eleonora Duse, Edmund Kean, Sarah Bernhardt and another Sarah, famous for her Lady Macbeth, Mrs. Siddons.

Mrs. Siddons stood in the wings through the whole performance until her entrance. Salvini would arrive at the theatre two hours early when he played *Othello*. He would just walk around inside. Then he would put on his make-up and continue walking. He then put on a part of his costume and walked around some more. These were preparations without the label. Many of these actors used preparations of their own device whether they knew of Stanislavski or not. As a matter of fact, Stanislavski's 'system' is based on his OBSERVATION and study of what great actors did to create the kind of work for which they were known.

We can break preparation down into three basic ideas or categories. First of all:

Instrument preparation...

Preparing your INSTRUMENT, yourself, to begin the scene. Take stock of what you need to do for yourself in order to enter the stage and play the scene. It might be as simple as not eating until after the show or as complex as doing preestablished physical and vocal warm ups.

Emotionally, it helps to take stock of exactly what's going on inside you, so you'll know what ADJUSTMENTS to make in order to play the scene. Are you nervous? Are you filled with tension? Where in the body is the tension? Are you sad or depressed, when the scene calls for the CHARACTER to be elated and passionate? Are you physically cramped and stiff when the character needs to be relaxed and fluid? The things that you do to and for yourself to go from one state to another are instrument preparation.

Use some RELAXATION techniques, some breathing exercises to calm yourself. Find your center. Deal with some of the conflicting feelings you might be experiencing before you begin the scene. If you're upset about something in your life and it is inappropriate for the scene, deal with it: first by acknowledging it and then by expressing it. Take care not to ignore these feelings or pretend to yourself that they're not important. In a way we're like calculators, in the sense that if we want to add a column of numbers, we must first 'clear' the calculator in order to get an accurate total. If you are going to build TRUTH, start with a foundation of truth in order to create a believable character.

Character preparation.

This can take from several minutes to hours to months. You may be required to use an accent, a limp, or some other physicalization for a part. For the movie *Godfather II*, Robert De Niro spent several weeks in Sicily to learn the DIALECT and MANNERISMS of the locals.

An actor who played the part of a stutterer in a film went to a speech therapist and learned to stutter. He observed video tapes of therapy, watched speech therapy sessions through two-way mirrors and practiced on un-suspecting people until he was believed. If you're playing a lawyer, you might visit your court house. You might even visit a law school.

If you're playing Richard III, in addition to all of the other elements of the scene, you must create the limp. You can work out an elaborate sensory choice to cause the limp or you can simply put your keys in your shoe. Presto! Instant limp!

You may be playing Ibsen in which case you should REHEARSE with clothing that will give you the same restric-tions as the clothes of the period. Women will wear long rehearsal skirts and blouses with high necklines. Men, if they are fops in a restoration comedy, will wear knickerlike pants and learn to walk in ways that exagger-ates their calf muscles. Women of the period found mens' calves very sexy. Men would wear upper garments that restricted their arm movements and gloves and lacy sleeve cuffs that would cause them to use their arms in a way that would protect their sleeves. Actors must work in rehearsal with wigs, beards, and mustaches and all kinds of external props and make-up appliances.

Emotional preparation.

You are responsible for creating the emotional life of the character. Does that statement make you nervous? It should. In one sense it's true. But in the creative artis-tic sense, it serves to create more tension and pressure on you than on a centipede trying to figure out how to mobilize all those legs to take a step. Remember, emo-tional life is a result. You're going to create the cause and trust yourself to pursue an action, then react.

If you've done your HOMEWORK and found personal choices that allow you to believe the circumstances, there will be natural 'triggers' to put you in touch with what you've found without going through all the steps that lead you to your original choices. In other words, you develop trust. Based on the circumstances and your RELATIONSHIP to the others in the play, you will have play-able actions. It is this combination of circumstances and actions that will give you your emotional life. If we try to have a particular emotion in life it will look fake. It's the same on the stage. In life we take action based on our perception of the situation we're in (circumstances).

91

Feelings and emotions accompany this. It's the same on the stage. There are however some things to consider.

Suppose you're playing Martha in Albee's *Who's Afraid of Virginia Woolf*. You create the circumstances. You feel that George has betrayed you. You choose an action, to indict George. The result is that you are genuinely filled with rage. So far so good. The problem might be that in your real life you've never been allowed to express any rage. You learned when you were young to suppress it whenever it came up as a survival tool. This strategy has led to your rage becoming repressed. Instead of thoroughly expressing the rage you actually feel, you cry. That is not the way Martha expresses rage according to Edward Albee and your director. That's the way *you* handle rage. Should this happen in a rehearsal you need to accept it, understand it and then work on some exercises that will teach your instrument to express rage directly. I'm not suggesting therapy. You don't need to know why you handle rage the way you do, or make any major life changes if you don't want to. You just need to be able to have a choice when you're on stage. Being an artist means being able to choose.

Where emotions are concerned there are no easy steps to follow that guarantee success. It's the same with art. If it were that finite it wouldn't be art, it would be science.

If you understand and create the given circumstances, and choose strong enough ACTIONS in order to pursue your OBJECTIVES, the emotions will come as a result of that process.

Prior Circumstances
The events in the play occurring before your scene or entrance that affect what you do. Sometimes called 'previous circumstances'.

Prior or previous circumstances, as they are sometimes called, deal with events before your CHARACTER'S appearance on stage. They are yet another way to examine a kind of theatrical cause and effect.

When you make an entrance in a scene, the audience has to believe that you're coming from the character's real life. If the audience for instance learns that your character got drunk the night before, then we need to see some evidence of that manifested in your be-havior. A hangover perhaps, or some indication that you were snockered several hours ago.

The text reference that your character was drunk sometime when he was off stage is a prior circumstance. Sometimes it's a GIVEN CIRCUMSTANCE as well.

If in the play we learn that the character broke up with his wife off stage, we need to see that behavior when he makes his entrance.

On a simpler more immediate level, you might be entering from an off stage kitchen. You might enter dry-ing your hands with a kitchen towel. If you're coming home from work, you can kick your shoes off and flop into a chair, or come in looking over your mail.

Part of your HOMEWORK is to find and create in the present the prior circumstances of the play. Once these are identified, they need to be incorporated into your PREPARATION. That creates the cause. Now you go on stage and respond in large part to those prior circumstances. That at least should be the effect.

Private Moment
An exercise developed by Lee Strasberg enabling an actor to focus concentration and behave privately in public.

Private moment is one of the METHOD'S most controversial exercises. It was developed by Lee Strasberg in 1956 and 1957 to aid actors in creating the ability to behave in a truly private fashion while being observed by an audi-ence. In other words, to be private in public.

The genesis of the idea came from Strasberg's study of STANISLAVSKI'S writings on what Stanislavski termed, 'public solitude'. Stanislavski postulated that if you could observe someone in private, in the simple act of brushing his hair, there would be an elegance associ-ated with it that we scarcely see in the theatre, except by the greats.

Based on this idea, Strasberg felt that acting was in part the ability to be private in public. He created the ex-ercise called private moment.

In the private moment exercise, a student chooses an ACTIVITY that for him or her, would be private. Not something personal, which you might keep on doing if someone came into the room, although you might be a bit embarrassed, but a CHOICE that's private. Something that you would stop doing if someone entered the room, even your husband or wife.

The student brings in personal props from home and SENSORILY creates the PLACE in the studio or classroom. This is usually done at the same time that other students are working on their exercises, which might not necessarily be private moments.

Lee Strasberg:

He then says, "I am going to choose the moment in this room when I think this particular thing about myself, when I worry about my home life or my relationship to people, when I carry on long speeches to people who aren't there, or dance wildly or sing or dress up or undress." He then does that moment as fully as he can, but he does not imitate. The doing is left to happen as easily as it can. He says, "I am going to see how far I can go in that direction. I will not do things that good taste obviously will not permit on the stage, but I will try to get close to my moment of privacy. If I get too close to a part that good taste does not permit, I will walk off stage. I'm not sure I'll reach that point, but if necessary I'll walk off and complete that part off stage and then come back. I will see what will happen. I will see if I can create it here as fully as if I were not being watched."[1]

The exercise is one that helps to focus CONCENTRATION on choice and the elements of the choice involved.

Strasberg claimed that for the private moment exercise no REHEARSAL was needed, because since it was a real activity from your life, it was something you've done before, and therefore rehearsal was built into it.

There are enormous benefits to be attained from private moment. The ability to sharpen focus and lessen the deleterious effects of the audience on the performance are only two. As you work with private moment

---

[1]*Strasberg At The Actors Studio*, Lee Strasberg and Robert Hethmon, (New York: Viking Press, 1965).

with a responsible teacher you will gain other benefits that will further help you customize your CRAFT.

WARNING: Unfortunately, some teachers and directors have abused the exercise.

A private moment exercise implies the presence of an audience. If you're being asked to do something questionable involving nudity or your sexuality for an audience of one, that's too private. There are many other responsible ways to deal with inhibitions and blocks that don't compromise your integrity or your dignity.

Projection
Sending the voice to all areas of the theatre.

The people who come together to watch a play are called the audience. They're not called spectators, but audience, from the word audio: hearing, listening. Shakespeare's CHARACTERS say they will 'hear a play'.

Obviously, if the actor doesn't project his voice the audience won't hear. The proposition sounds simple enough, yet there are two schools of thought on the subject.

The first school says the audience must hear the play. Playwrights and directors usually agree. Sometimes, however, a teacher or director will allow an actor to continue at a normal volume, even risking being unheard by the audience, because the actor is becoming INVOLVED for perhaps the first time. One doesn't want to interfere in this stage of the actor's development. At this point the connection to the other actors on stage, the total belief in TASKS set, and the beginning of TRUTHFUL behavior are what is wanted as a base for the actor's study and/or performance.

When directing a play, the director takes into account the level of performer and which week of REHEARSAL he's in. If the director can't hear an actor whom he knows is good and capable of being heard, he may give NOTES on projection. Especially if it's in the final weeks of rehearsal. When an experienced, good actor doesn't project, it's sometimes due to SELF INDULGENCE. A good director will call him on it and/or give the actor an ADJUSTMENT.

Strasberg felt that concerning himself with projection too early would lead to a less than TRUTHFUL performance.

On the other hand, I remember seeing a friend, an Academy Award nominee, in a Broadway production. His performance was stunning, but there were times that he couldn't be heard. And I was sitting in the front of the house. There were also reviews that said he couldn't be heard. After the show I asked him about his lack of projection. His answer was, "I'm doing the work. There's a full character up there. Sometimes in life you don't hear every word."

An actor's intentional lack of projection is the exception not the rule. The audience has a right to hear all of the playwright's words. Except in this instance it was the artists CHOICE. And the performance was great. I later saw a performance with another well-known actor who took over the role. I heard every word. The performance though was not memorable.

Proscenium
Literally, before the scenery. The stage or playing area in front of the scenery. The arch above the stage is also called the proscenium arch.

In ancient Greek and Roman times, proscenium referred to the stage itself. It was in front of or before the scenery. In modern times it is the part of the stage in front of the curtain.

A proscenium theatre is one in which the audience is seated in front of the stage.

A proscenium arch is the arch that extends above the stage from STAGE LEFT to STAGE RIGHT.

Psychological Gesture
A concept/exercise invented by Michael Chekhov that asks the actor to find one or more sweeping gestures that encapsulates the goal of the character.

Psychological gesture is described in detail in Michael Chekhov's[1] *To the Actor.*[2] Chekhov found that the right physical gesture can tap into our own psychology, our feelings, and our will power. The gesture is movement and movement is action.

If you are working for a particular kind of CHARACTER, one who is open, honest, filled with love and trust, you can find for yourself a gesture, a movement that will coax

96

those feelings already in you to the surface. Chekhov said that in performance the actor may never actually exhibit the psychological gesture. But having done it in REHEARSAL or in PREPARATION, the feelings and emotions begin to shape the behavior. In his book there are many examples of behaviors and correspondent characters, with accompanying drawings of actual psychological gestures and instructions and exercises on how to work with them.

Recently there have been some clinical psychological studies that show emotions can be generated by placing your face in the same physical position as when you really experienced those feelings. Actual points on the face have been mapped out showing the elicitation of pain, sorrow, fear, hate, love, etc. Experiments have shown that re-creating those facial points stimulates the actual emotion.

To actors, this idea sounds exciting, as they are always seemingly looking to *feel*. Feeling, however, is not as much of the actors' problem as the expression of feeling.

Psychological gesture can be a valuable explorative and/or preparative technique if used responsibly. That is to say, do not use it in an attempt to go for the end result. Rather use it to EXPLORE the process of MOMENT TO MOMENT behavior where the correct results are a byproduct of correct work and trust in your CRAFT.

---

[1] Michael Chekhov (1891–1955) was the nephew of playwright Anton Chekhov. In the words of STANISLAVSKI, "Michael Chekhov is my most brilliant pupil." Chekhov worked with the Moscow Art Theatre as an actor. He then formulated his own teaching ideas based on Stanislavski's 'system'. He had several studios in America where he worked on bringing joy and fun back to 'the work'. He devised many exercises designed to free the actor using IMAGINATION, movement, 'feeling of ease', 'personal atmosphere', and CONCENTRATION.

[2] *To the Actor* (New York: Harper and Row Publishers, Inc., 1953).

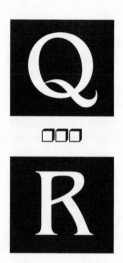

Rehearsal

The process of making ready a play or presentation by repetition and exploration.

The Middle English spelling of rehearsal, as it exists in Henslowe's Diary of 1599,[1] is rehearsall. As there was no formal knowledge of spelling in those days (words were spelled phonetically) we might infer more about rehearsals by looking at the origins of the word. If you break it down, it could have been: re-hears-all, or, about hearing all, all over again. In French rehearsal is translated as repetition, but in German the word means to probe. As we learn to rehear, repeat, and probe, we enter into the stage door of theatre magic.

There are two different approaches to the way today's plays are rehearsed by directors—and to the ways that actors adapt to those approaches.

One method begins by sitting down with the actors for a first reading and a discussion of the play. This might continue for two or three days, during which time the director will outline his concept of how he sees the play, show scenic designs, analyze the play, and deal with TEXT work. Then comes 'getting it up on its feet', with IMPROVISATIONS, and EXPLORATION. During the second half

---

[1] Philip Henslowe was a producer and manager of The Rose Playhouse which existed in London not far from Shakespeare's Globe Theatre. He kept a diary that survives to give us some of our best information on the Elizabethan theatre.

of the rehearsal period, the director will be concerned with BLOCKING and 'teching' the show up until final dress rehearsal.

Other directors work differently. They might start by blocking the play immediately. They have done so much pre-production with the designers (set, lighting, sound, costume, etc.) that they know exactly what they're after well before the first actor is hired.

The decision of which way to direct the play has to do for the most part with how the director was trained or the STYLE or subject of the play itself. This will have an effect on casting. A more performance oriented actor will usually be cast in the play that will be blocked immediately and will be 'off book' as soon as possible.

A METHOD trained director tends to work with 'process oriented' actors. Actually, whichever discipline is chosen, a process is involved. In this case, actors will be asked to read simply, ask questions, IMPROVISE, EXPLORE, and not learn lines right away so as not to get stuck in PATTERNS.

Many books on directing deal with using exploration in rehearsal. This is crucial. Your rehearsal process as an actor is one of finding every CHOICE you can that you absolutely, positively know will *not* work. What you're left with is what you know for sure will work.

One thing actors should keep in mind when beginning rehearsals is setting specific goals for themselves to accomplish in each session. It's something you expect of the director, why not of the actor. Good actors have goals and problems that they want to work out automatically. New or less experienced actors often wait to be told what to do. This is an excuse for not doing HOMEWORK. Homework means going over OBJECTIVES, finding the OBSTACLES, analyzing MOTIVATIONS, working on TEXT, etc. When you've done this, it's easier to know what you want to do in rehearsal. It may even coincide with exactly what the director wants.

Relationship
The connection between your character and the other characters in the play.

First let's talk about relating—period. When we have an understanding of how to do that on the stage or in front of a camera, we can then take a closer look at the quality and judgments of relationships.

In life there are people we relate to instantly and some we can't relate to at all. Sometimes we meet a person who comes from a different geographical place, and we find it hard to relate to him. Sometimes the fact that his origins are different is what makes him attractive to us. In any case, the common denominator in relating to someone is to get outside of your own head and extend yourself into the other person. Pay attention to him. Put the focus on him. Wonder, watch, and guess about him.

You can often spot new or untrained actors by a kind of self-consciousness. They *wonder* alright, but about things in relation to themselves. They ask, "Do I look okay? Will I remember my mark, my lines, my STAGE BUSINESS? Did my friends show up, or the agent I invited?" With all that energy focused on them, it's a wonder they have any left for you.

There are some obvious questions to help you with CHARACTER relationships. The first one is, are you related to the other characters: your mother, father, sister, brother. Whether they're related to you or not, how do you, or rather, how does your character feel about them. You could hate your dad and love your cousin, or you might love your mom and be furious with her.

Whatever the relationship with whomever you're acting, you will need to make SPECIFIC, personal CHOICES. If you use the techniques of ENDOWMENT, SUBSTITUTION or PERSONALIZATION, the relationship will grow. It will grow from the genuine seeds that you've carefully sown.

Some actors are so gifted as imitators that they forego the above PREPARATION. The audience often 'gets it' right away. But they get it through their understanding only. They even think in their heads, "Oh, I get it. She's his daughter."

When you take the risks and do the advance work on yourself and the other character, in terms of a true relationship that is personal to you, you will have created in your partner a cause that will affect you on a deeper level. Your relationships will be unique, focused, and they will have power. They will be alive and compelling for an audience to watch. That's something to which all actors can relate.

Relaxation
The process of removing or reducing tension in the muscles and stress in the instrument.

True creativity happens at the point of relaxation. STANISLAVSKI and the Moscow Art Theatre made much of relaxation in teaching, acting and directing. Stanislavski felt that when an actor was tense, he would be prevented from expressing small, INSTINCTIVE, detailed gestures. On the other hand, Vakhtangov[1] said that the lack of relaxation lead to what we now call actors 'ticks'. Drumming fingers unconsciously, shaking your leg, playing with your hair, etc., are all MANNERISMS that come from the actor, not the CHARACTER. That can confuse an audience if the character is supposed to be relaxed and the actor playing him is nervously biting his lip, unaware.

It's really common sense. Who wants to be stressed out and nervous let alone perform that way? But it is important to know how to let the tension out and the creativity in.

First know whether you're tense or not. In every acting class there are actors who swear they're relaxed when they're not. When you point this out and show them how to alleviate it, they act more easily and better.

There are many ways to reduce stress and relax. The right way is the way that works best for you. What follows is *a* way to relax, not *the* way. Try this:

> Sit comfortably in a chair so that you could fall asleep. Use a chair without arms (in the studio we use ordinary folding chairs). Let your head fall backwards or forwards and let your arms fall by your sides. Or lie down on the floor on your back. Get comfortable. Close your eyes gently. Think sleep. Now, in your mind, take a physical inventory of all your muscle groups to see if any tension is there.

---

[1] Evgeny Vakhtangov was a student of Stanislavski and a great director in his own right. Vakhtangov, in agreement with Stanislavski, wanted inward truth from the actor, however, he was interested in displaying that truth in very stylized productions. Unconscious 'ticks', according to Vakhtangov, interfered with the precision necessary in staging his stylized productions.

Start at the feet. Ask yourself, *is there any ten-sion in the muscles of my feet?* Visualize a magic beam of light or simply warm, pleasant sunshine washing over your feet to relax them. Then slowly and systematically move the beam over your body from toe to head. Go to your calves, check for tension. Move to your thighs, buttocks, abdomen, stomach, chest or pectoral muscles, shoulders and arms. Check the hands, fingers and thumbs for tension. If you do discover tension in a muscle group, simply let go. Send a command from the brain to relax that area. When you've scanned all the muscles groups below the neck, focus your attention on 'emotional ten-sion' above the neck.

There are four basic areas of emotional ten-sion. First the temples, secondly, the fore-head, eyebrow, and bridge of the nose area, then the eyes and eyelids, and finally the jaw, the throat, the tongue, and mouth. Your jaw should be slackened more than you may think necessary. Your lips should be parted about half an inch. Let any thoughts you may have travel from one side of the mind, so to speak, to the other. Try not to dwell on any one thought.

Here's another way: In a chair or on the floor as above, place one hand palm down on your stomach (above your bellybutton) and the other hand palm down on your chest.
Now breath in through the nose, fully inflating your lungs, counting eight seconds in and ex-pelling the air through the mouth, eight sec-onds out. As you take a breath in, distend your stomach so that it physically rises and presses against your hand. As you release the breath and exhale, your stomach should vis-ibly fall. Visualize any tension leaving on your breath when you exhale. Your hand is on your chest to monitor it so that it doesn't move at all. Your chest should stay still. Do five or six

of these breaths. Consider in and out as one breath.

If, after this there is still some tension in a particular muscle group, do a 'tense and relax' exercise. Focus on the tense area (e.g. shoulder), tense it up as hard as you can and hold for six seconds while holding your breath. At the end of six seconds release your breath slowly, visualizing the tension leaving on your breath for another six seconds. Repeat this tense and relax five or six times.

Your muscles have spent years learning how to respond to and deal with tension-making stimuli. The tense and relax exercise is a way to teach the muscles how to relax physically. Practice and the relaxation will happen more quickly each time.

It is part of your job as an artist to be able to relax and produce a tension-free performance. Experiment. Find your own way. Learn your own 'triggers' of where you hold your tension. Sometimes when discussing business on the phone you can do a quick muscle scan and discover that perhaps your shoulders are tense. When you drop your shoulders (the trigger) and allow the relaxation in, the quality of the phone call can dramatically change for the better. Relax. As the song says, "Don't worry, be happy."

Repetition

An exercise developed by Sanford Meisner called the Word Repetition Game to enable students to work spontaneously off one another and follow instinctive impulses.

"I want you to do this exercise." "You want me to do this exercise." "Yes, I want you to do this exercise." "You want me to." "I want you to."

The above is an example of 'repetition', an exercise that forms the basis of what is called the Meisner Technique, named after Sanford Meisner. Meisner was an original member of The Group Theatre in the 1930s. He has trained many stars in New York at The Neighborhood Playhouse, where he has headed the acting department for over forty years.

The repetition exercise, as it's more commonly known, is a long process. Students begin repetition and continue with variations and additions for over a year. Different 'Meisner' teachers vary the way in which it is taught.

To begin, two actors sit facing each other in front of the class. One simply makes a statement about something he finds interesting in the other. "You have brown eyes." The other actor just listens and repeats exactly what she hears, "You have brown eyes." Now the first actor listens and repeats again. And so on. What you have gained from the work up to this point is something mechanical. There is no humanness in it. However, there is a real connection between two people. In isn't acted. It's genuine. That's something!

Now take the example at the top of this page. In the third repetition, "Yes, I want you to do this exercise". It's not simply or accurately repeated. Somebody added the word "Yes" to the basic repetition. Somebody added a point of view. The addition of that point of view made the exchange less mechanical, more human. It created the potential for emotion. For behavior.

Now, what did the actors actually do? They listened. They repeated what they heard. Then they added their own point of view. The reality became the doing and the doing became reality. The attention was shifted off the actor and onto his partner. There was no INDICATING or imitating of doing, just the reality of doing.

As the work progresses you will learn to follow your INSTINCT and include that response in the repetition. The teacher will monitor the exercise to make sure you don't deviate from instinctively 'doing' by going into your head. By thinking! Most acting exercises you will ever do are not thinking exercises. Thinking is passive. Doing is active. Acting is doing.

As the repetition continues more elements are added. Things such as independent physical ACTIVITY which incorporates a TASK that is difficult or impossible to do are vital.

The technique allows you to focus your CONCENTRATION outside yourself, work from your INSTINCT, and not to 'do' unless and until something really happens to you. It will teach you to create TRUTH. It will teach me to create truth? Yes, I said truth. Truth? Truth!

Rhythm

The systematic impression and expression of artistic stimuli, continually swinging, as does a pendulum, back and forth, so that both extremes exist to create a moving or pulsating whole.

Rhythm is at the core of nature, life, and creativity. Can you remember your first look at an amoeba under a microscope? Here is a one-celled animal with a nucleus, a cell membrane, and cytoplasm and it has its own rhythm. This is the common denominator between all living things, all created and creative things.

What is an artist's definition of rhythm? "The orderly, measurable changes of all the different elements comprised in a work of art – provided that all those changes progressively stimulate the attention of the spectator and lead invariably to the final aim of the artist." That is the best definition of rhythm that I've ever heard discussed. It's taken from Richard Boleslavsky's, *ACTING: The First Six Lessons*.[1]

All things, Boleslavsky[2] teaches us, have rhythm. This is not to be confused with TEMPO, which is limited by comparison. A glacier moves two inches in a century while a humming bird might flap its wings a hundred times in a second.

Each emotion, CHARACTER, and character mood has a different rhythm. They are all facets of one gem, with one unique frequency. We can learn by OBSERVING rhythms first. It's probably easiest with music where rhythm is most pronounced. Observe and allow yourself to get caught up in the different changes of rhythm and resultant changes of your emotions.

Realize, however, that these rhythms are the result *not* the process. If you settle on the rhythm of the ocean, the waves for instance, what rhythm will that be? A stormy ocean? A calm, pacific ocean? Allow that rhythm

---

[1] *ACTING: The First Six Lessons*, by Richard Boleslavsky (New York: Theatre Arts Books, 1933).

[2] Richard Boleslavsky and Maria Ouspenskaya opened the American Laboratory Theatre teaching the works of Stanislavski in New York in the 1920s. Boleslavsky was Lee Strasberg's teacher.

to enter you and change your own rhythm of the moment. Now express yourself with your new rhythm. See how it affects the TEXT. See what clues in the text (GEAR CHANGES) will help you find the best rhythm. Look carefully at cause and effect when focusing on your CHOICE of rhythm. When we are agitated or excited our breathing quickens, even if we are still. Create the cause, the stimulus, and you will discover the right rhythm.

In acting, rhythm does not come only from nature. It comes from nature via the playwright. If, as an actor your job is to create a believable role, then in order to do that, look to the creator of the character, the playwright. Any character created by a writer will contain that writer's rhythm. Boleslavsky, "A good writer's fool is no more foolish than his creator's mind, and a prophet no more wise than the man who conceived him."

Scansion

According to Webster's, scansion is, "the analysis of verse to show its meter." See also VERSE TECHNIQUE.

A metric line of verse is made up of metric feet. There are different types of metric feet. They are:

Anapest:	– –/	Two weak syllables followed by a strong one.
Dactyl	/– –	One strong syllable followed by two weak.
Trochee	/–	One strong followed by one weak.
Iamb	–/	One weak followed by one strong.
Spondee	//	Two strong syllables together.

These metric feet can be grouped in specific numbers per line. Five iambs per line would be called 'iambic pentameter':

"Is this—the face—that launched—a thou -
sand ships"

Four trochees per line would be trochaic quadrimeter, etc.

"Double,—double—toil and—trouble;
Fire—burn and—cauldron—bubble."

Scansion is a process that is used by poets to understand and analyze poetry or verse better. They actually write in the accent stresses (slashes and dashes) above the words in the text.

Although some playwrights write in verse, SHAKESPEARE for one, the actor does not have to literally scan each line in order to act it. Now before all the college professors throw this book out of their respective windows, let me state that verse and meter should be construed by the actor to be an acting note from the playwright. Actors must acknowledge the verse and not attempt to smooth it out into prose. If the playwright had wanted to express him or herself in prose, he or she would have.

Use the clues that you uncover from the verse as stimuli to help you make CHOICES that tell the play's story.

Scene Study

Utilizing a scene with two or more people to learn specific acting techniques to develop and refine a craft.

Doing a scene in class is the toughest acting you will ever have to do. First of all, you're presenting your scene to your peers. They know you, and they know what you're trying to do. Secondly, you are struggling to use and master one or more techniques that you've learned in class. Thirdly, you have no director. Finally, and most importantly, you don't have time. You have three or four rehearsals in one or two weeks time and you expect to have the same results as a finished performance in a show that you've rehearsed every day all day for four weeks. It ain't gonna happen!

The result of scene study is the assimilation of your CRAFT. It is not to have a finished performance. That is why in the phrase 'scene study', the operative word is *study*.

After a scene is played in the studio, the two actors remain on stage. They will usually explain what it is that they've worked for. That is, what did they want to accomplish? How did they interpret the situation, the CHARACTERS and their respective OBJECTIVES? What CHOICES did they make to produce the behavior observed by the class?

The critique is usually based on what the actors said that they worked on. It is a reflection of whether or not their TASKS were successfully executed. Did the choices work? Did we believe the behavior? Did we understand the material? These are all questions that must be addressed in order to make the necessary ADJUSTMENTS to improve the actors' technique.

If your scene was assigned by your teacher, try to ascertain why this particular scene was chosen for you. Is it simply a matter of your TYPE? Or is there something that this scene will teach you? Perhaps the scene focuses more on RELATIONSHIP. Or the lesson might be in SENSE MEMORY. If you can get an idea of why you're doing the scene, you can focus your work on those SPECIFIC points.

Make scene study important! It's still the best way to learn your CRAFT. Have goals ready when you REHEARSE. Avoid talking to death about the scene. Sure, some talk is necessary. Is the scene indoors or outdoors? Is it hot or cold? Where are the doors and windows? Where is the mirror? These must be agreed upon from the beginning, so talk is appropriate. However you never need to discuss with anyone your choices of ACTION, SUBSTITUTION, PERSONALIZATION, etc. Even in class, we don't need to know about a choice in terms of names, dates or places. We're interested in the behavior only! Keep what's private, private! Use GIBBERISH or random numbers to express your personal choices before you're ready to plug the choice into the TEXT.

In our class structure we repeat the same scene an average of three times. Any more than that and actors may become stale and/or performance oriented. Any less and actors don't have enough time to apply the CRITIQUE. Usually two weeks will elapse between scene dates.

If you can make the time, have more than one scene going all the time. Be greedy with your class time. There will always be students who hang out in the back of the class and there will always be actors who tend towards the front. Be an actor, think like an actor. Do as many scenes as you can, as often as you can.

Self Indulgence
Acting for a catharsis instead of an audience.

Excuse me, I 'catharted'! Everyone enjoys the relief of a cathartic experience. There is turmoil, then there is release. It's personal because it's most profoundly experienced by the one who has the catharsis. When actors experience a personal release of long held emotions in an acting class (BREAKTHROUGHS), they sometimes become 'addicted' to the exercise work that got them there. It feels good to feel good. They start using the CRAFT to affect themselves instead of the audience. They act to indulge themselves.

The problem is that people who fall into self indulgent acting generally aren't aware of it. They even think that what they did was good. Because they 'felt' it. Well, surprise, it's the audience who's supposed to feel it.

Every so often you will see an actor in class (it's usually female) who will cry real tears (every acting class has a crier.) Real pain is coming up in this real human being and we sit there and think, "Oh shut up already." Why should we feel hostility to someone's real pain? Because the pain is created to affect only her. It is not to be shared with us. It's as if she's saying *This pain is so deep and so profound that you people can't possibly help me.* We pick up that message and think, *Okay, then the hell with you!*

When you make CHOICES and, as a result, an emotion rises in you, it's to be expressed, not impressed. It needs to be released, not withheld. This is not to be confused with 'sitting on' a feeling, which is often very effective in a scene.

In real life we're often affected by strong emotions that, because of the situation, we choose not to express. When you are truly feeling an emotion that your CHARACTER wants to withhold in order to pursue his OBJECTIVE, (you don't want your partner to know what you're feeling but you certainly need the audience to know) then you can 'sit on', or 'cap' the emotion.

Have you heard these two different schools of thoughts on acting? One school says, "Let it all hang out. Don't hold anything back," and the other school says, "Don't give 'em everything. Hold back a little bit for mystery." They're both right. As an actor you need the INSTRUMENTAL flexibility to be able to let it all hang out. But if you do express everything in your biggest moment, from that point on the audience will know that there is no more than that. Hold back a little bit, only by choice. That's the difference. Choice is what enables us to call ourselves artists.

Sense Memory
Re-creating experience and belief through the memory of the five senses. Creating a sensory response to a non-existing object.

What is it?

Sense Memory is a way of using your five senses to 'record' various stimuli (HOT SENSATIONS, COLD SENSATIONS, an inanimate OBJECT, an illness, the SHARP TASTE of a lemon, a person, etc.), and 'play them back' so that your senses actually respond to things that are not really there.

Sense memory is a technique that will allow you to believe what the CHARACTER believes. It is not a technique that is used to create emotional behavior. This point cannot be overstressed. The characters you play aren't trying to have emotions, they're trying to do something, to accomplish an OBJECTIVE. We are talking about using and trusting a process, not going directly for a result.

Why do we do it?

As an actor you strive for TRUTH and believability in your work. You want your character to behave with full, powerful emotions. Where do the emotions come from? How are emotions created? And, is creating emotions the most effective way to render truth?

STANISLAVSKI says that emotions come from a combination of two concepts. They are ACTION and belief in the GIVEN CIRCUMSTANCES of the play. Actions, once they are well defined, can be pursued, but how do you make yourself believe something that's not real?

"How is sucking a lemon going to make me a better actor?" actors usually wonder when they first hear about sensory work. If you can suck the lemon and re-create the responses later on without the actual lemon, you're creating a reality that no longer exists. You're learning to trust your INSTRUMENT to react without any intellectual interference. It may sound simple, but there are actors out there who ignore their own natural, ORGANIC responses to something and express themselves in a contrived manner. It's like burning your finger and instead of instantly expressing the pain, working out the best and most theatrical way to say, "Ouch!"

If you try to create a past experience by trying to remember it, picture it or IMAGINE it, you engage in an intellectual exercise. In other words you go into your head.[1]

Trying to remember an experience intellectually doesn't work as well as sense memory because the original experience becomes clouded by how your head made order out of it. Let's say you want to EXPLORE grief by 'using' the loss of your dog or cat. Other factors, such as the your ability to cope with loss, your belief in life after death, and your upbringing in terms of how you relate to animals or pets affect the expression of those behaviors. These factors can lead to inconsistencies in expressing the behavior of the character. The audience can get sidetracked. Whose story are you playing, the character's or your own? And, if you're using yourself as the character, how are you going to recall a CHOICE if not through your intellectual memory?

Be sense-able. You can investigate past behaviors without resorting to the total use of your intellect. Your senses have a memory of their own.

How does it Work?
Sense memory works by using the principles of Pavlovian conditioning. There is evidence showing that

---

[1] Many actors will tell you they can just imagine what they need to accomplish in a role, and they can make it work. If you question them further, however, about their choices, you find that a natural sensory process happens in the course of their imagining what they want to 'use'.

If for any reason your imagination is not responsive on a given day you can always count on sense memory, a variation of human conditioned response.

Stanislavski knew of Pavlov's work in human conditioned response and human conditioned reflex.

Dr. Ivan Pavlov conditioned a dog to salivate when exposed to the sound of a metronome during the dog's exposure to food.[2] After a time all that was needed to get the dog to salivate was to play the metronome. In a sense (no pun intended), Dr. Pavlov's dog was one of the first Method actors. The dog was responding truthfully to a stimulus that was not real.

Any personal experience you have ever wanted to use in order to discover more about a character first came to you through your senses. If you won an award, you heard your introduction, you heard applause, you saw people, shapes, and colors. You touched different textures, from shaking the hand of the presenter to feeling tactually the award itself. You smelled fresh paint near the stage and tasted the breath mint on which you relied. Then your head made order out of the experience, depending on the events that shaped your life.

[2] **Experiment 1.**

Pavlov placed a dog in a standard experimental situation. On repeated *conditioning* trials, a tone was sounded for 5 seconds, and approximately 2 seconds later the dog was given powdered food. This pairing of tone and food powder was repeated, with trials spaced from 5 to 35 minutes apart at random intervals, for fifty trials. Trials 1, 10, 20, 30, 40, and 50 were *test* trials, that is, the tone was sounded for 30 seconds and *no* food powder was given. The results, in part, were: In trial #10, the dog produced 6 drops of saliva and the time between the onset of the tone and salivation was 18 seconds. In trial #50, the dog produced 59 drops of saliva in 2 seconds.

Experiment 2.

A dog had been conditioned to salivate to a metronome beating at 104 ticks per minute. Several interspersed test trials (metronome ticking for 30 seconds but not followed by food powder) provided approximately 10 drops of saliva on each trial. The ticking metronome was then presented on every trial for 30 seconds without being paired with food powder. (Sufficient time was allowed between trials to avoid appreciable fatigue.) The results of this series of consecutive trials without food are presented below, in part:

In trial number 1, the dog produced 10 drops of saliva in 3 seconds between onset of metronome & salivation. There were 9 trials, producing successively fewer drops of saliva in progressively higher numbers of seconds. *

* *The Analysis of Behavior* by James G. Holland and B. F. Skinner (New York: McGraw-Hill Book Company, Inc., 1961).

Perhaps you can remember your first kiss. Can your nose remember your lover's scent? Can your eyes remember the highlights in your sweetheart's hair? Can your skin recall the climate of the outdoors or indoors? What sounds do your ears remember? Do your neck and shoulder muscles remember what position they were in? No, you say? Well you can train them to remember. That is sensory training.

Have you ever been in a crowd, gotten a whiff of someone's after-shave or cologne and then instantly you're transported back to another time and place? If you have, you were experiencing the power of your sense memory. By tapping into your sense memory you will gain consistency in your TASK of believing and put IN-SPIRATION into your work.

Sense memory training is usually accomplished in an acting class where the student works on a different sensory exercise each week. Strasberg gave the exercises in a particular order. You would begin with MORNING DRINK where you sensorily created your own breakfast beverage (coffee, tea, or milk, etc.). You did it by using the real object at home, daily, and asking questions about the object, as if you've never experienced the object before. Again, these should be questions that can be answered by your senses. You would then move on to other exercises such as THE MIRROR, which includes putting on make-up or shaving, SUNSHINE and then into SHARP PAIN , which often evokes emotional behavior. These exercises would be followed by SHARP TASTE, SHARP SMELL, taking a SHOWER/BATH, and then you would start working with a PERSONAL OBJECT, then two objects at a time (one INTERNAL and one EXTERNAL), and then on to PRIVATE MOMENT.

As you progress, you begin combining exercises. You may be instructed to work on 'taste' and 'itch', first working on one and then having your teacher switch you to the other. Your teacher may switch you back and forth before asking you to work on both at the same time. This is called 'twos'. You then go on to 'threes', switching and combining three different exercises; and on to 'four's'. If you think about it, in real life we are always doing 'fives.' We are continually operating on all five senses. That's what we strive for on the stage too.

There is another kind of progression that occurs with actors who are just beginning to learn sensory. Deep down, their negative, skeptical side doesn't really believe all this sensory stuff. They say to themselves, *It seems to make sense and the other people sure seem* IN-VOLVED *but, gee, I don't know... I don't really believe this is a cup of coffee. It's just air. We're just pantomiming, pretending. Well, I like everything else in the class. I'll just pretend to do it. I'll go along with it.*

Then, as you work from week to week, you start to become more and more relaxed. Your muscular 'armour' comes down a little. In about the fourth or fifth week you're up to SHARP PAIN, working routinely, and then all of a sudden BANG! The pain really takes hold. You know you don't really have a pain, but by God you're responding to pain exactly as if it were real. You sense that it is real. It's like waking a herd of sleeping elephants within you.

Some people, men especially, experience a kind of 'pins and needles' reaction in the lips, face, arms, hands, and fingers. Every so often the feeling is so strong you can see panic in the actor's eyes. This is a brand new experience for him. He has nothing to compare it to. Sometimes when this happens the teacher will have to move his hands and fingers for him and urge him to express what's happening through vocal sounds from the diaphragm. Sound is the vehicle for expression. If the feeling isn't expressed through the sound, it will stay in the arms, fingers, face, etc. Now the actor experiences and respects the power of sensory work. He must, however, do the requisite INSTRUMENT work in order to be able to process what he's created.

In order to have results like this you must do the HOMEWORK. It's important to find a place to work on your CRAFT for about an hour a day. Singers and dancers warm up their voices and limber up their bodies; so too must actors work out every day. Respect your craft. Homework is your 'recording' of the stimulus for 'playback' later on.

How do you do it?

Ask a child to make believe he has a book and he will employ the technique of pretending. His task becomes one of pretending he has a book, not creating the reality of a book. As you watch, you will certainly get the idea. You will also find it entertaining in most cases, because of the naiveté and simplicity with which the child goes about pretending. Chances are you will not believe the child believes he has a real book.

That's because a child's CONCENTRATION and attention are focused on making believe and not on making real. The fact that it *isn't* true is what the child builds on. Because we all began as children, we INSTINCTIVELY try to believe or pretend in order to answer the demands of the play. Rather than building on what is not real, you can 'program' your creativity by focusing on what is. You can use your senses to 'record' what's real and 'playback' what you've recorded. You do it by concentrating on specific details of the object you're creating.

The way you focus your attention on the object is the way you ask questions about it. Your questions imply the object exists. Once you begin the process of questioning or exploring the object, you will have fixed your concentration on the object as a byproduct of the questioning process. If for example you want to create your favorite piece of music, you would ask a question like, *What happens in my body when I hear this music?* The answer your body gives you is to dance. You dance. Your ears begin to remember the sound of the music. If however you say to yourself, *I hear my favorite music*, then chances are your self (that is, your truth sense) would respond, *No you don't. There's no music here*.

Try this: ask yourself how heavy this book is. Not in ounces (that's a head answer), but how much muscle power do you need to hold it? Do you need one hand or two? How much of your vision does the book obscure? How does the light affect it? Does the book cast any shadows? How much light do the shadows obscure? How much space does it take up between your fingers? Now ask your eyes, muscles, and fingers to remember the book. Good. Put the book down, behind you, let's say. Go back to the same physical position you were in when you started this experiment. Do your muscles recall the weight of the book? Can your eyes remember it's colors, its size, the shadows, other sensory idiosyncrasies? That's sense memory! It can be that easy!

How do you use it?

You use it by employing and trusting the process that it teaches you. The most creative uses of sense memory are not the literal ones you do in class on a weekly basis. What you use are the results you get from those exercises. That's not to say you will go directly for the result. Rather you will use many of the processes that get you to each of the respective results. You will trust your powers of observation and your sense of wonder and curiosity. They in turn will stimulate your concentration. That will allow you to create and combine stimuli, the effects of which you've already begun to explore.

You don't need to become a fanatic or a perfectionist about using it to create a book or a phone, for instance. If you need to use a book on stage, they'll get you a real one. It's the same with a phone, a drink, or any prop, you get to work with the real thing. If the *style* of the production demands that you create it without the actual object, you will be able to.

There are acting techniques that stress working totally off the other person. They work brilliantly until you take the other person away, as in doing a MONOLOGUE. In television and film you might have a scene where you pour your heart out to your scene partner, but on the day of your close-up your partner isn't even on the set. You'd better know how to create her. Use sensory when you need to create seeing something visual taking place off stage or over the audiences heads. Use it to really smell the bouquet of flowers your leading man gives you. Use it to feel the effects of the 'champagne' you're drinking. Use some of the sensory TASKS as CHOICES for a PREPARATION.

You're training your senses so you will be able to create any reality when you need to. That is what actors get paid to do. If you can create the book, you can create Hamlet's castle; you can create the engagement ring your lover gives you. You can create anything. And you will respond to what you create. You will believe what you create and so will the audience.

As you experiment with different stimuli you will find other ways to use this all important creative tool.

NOTE There are individual sensory exercises alphabetically listed beginning on the following page. They are classic exercises. Two that we do in the classes at Drama Project are not classics. We have added them to the repertoire.

Rapid Fire
After you have gained proficiency with all of the sensory exercises, including combining more than one at the same time, (two's, three's and four's), try 'rapid fire'. There is no homework for rapid fire. Your teacher se-

lects about four or five different sensory exercises such as smell, itch, taste, drunk and sharp pain. When others in the class start their respective exercises, you are given one exercise from the 'rapid fire' group. When you are involved with the object, your teacher will tell you to "Drop it (the particular exercise you're working on) and pick up 'taste'," or whatever the next one in the sequence is. You spend about ten or fifteen minutes on each exercise in the rapid fire group. There is a value in going immediately from one stimulus to another, on command, without preparation.

Sudden Death

Sudden Death is similar to 'rapid fire' above except you don't 'drop' the current exercise and move on to the next. Instead you keep adding exercises in the predetermined 'sudden death' group (four or five prepicked objects). You are systematically combining all of the objects by the end of the sudden death exercise. When advanced actors 'survive' the sudden death exercise, they exhibit a confidence that ultimately translates to their scene work. If you can fulfill the demands of sudden death, there isn't much else to worry you.

The Exercises

The following is a list of the *classic* sense memory exercises. You can work on one per week, devoting about an hour a day to each TASK.

•Cold Sensation

A sense-memory exercise in which you create, or record, a specific cold sensation in your senses for playback at a later time.

Cold, as in the other sensory exercises, first involves exploring actual cold sensations as they apply to you physically. Why do we want to create cold in the first place? Well, not just to portray cold accurately, but very often some extremely powerful behavior will arise from EXPLORING cold. You could use this as a CHOICE for a PREPARATION that is unrelated to the weather. Some actors will work on cold, and what results is fear or anxiety stemming from an early childhood experience. Cold is also an excellent INSTRUMENT

117

exercise. If you make a large choice regarding the cold (i.e. the Arctic in winter without a shirt on, as opposed to being in an air conditioned room wearing a sweater) your instrument will stretch because you will have that much more to express both physically and vocally.

In working on the exercise itself, begin by first sense-memorizing the actual cold sensation. Find a SPECIFIC cold place. It can be a very cold day in which you simply go outside without your coat (not for too long, please be *sensible*) or if it's summer, perhaps you know an actor who works in a restaurant and can get you into a walk-in refrigerator. Also, you might visit the frozen food section of your super market to experience the cold sensation.

Once you've found your cold sensation, begin by asking questions that pertain to your senses. On what part of my face do I feel the cold first? The tip of my nose? My ears? How does my breathing change? How deeply can I take the cold into my lungs? What happens when I relax my body while shivering? Do I speak softer or louder? Again, the direction that's inherent in all sensory work is to keep asking questions that relate to your senses as opposed to your 'head'. In other words the answer to how cold my nose is should not be thirty-seven degrees, but as cold as my nose says it is. My nose has the answer not my intellect.

Once you *believe* the cold, that is your senses responding to the memory of the cold, make sure you are expressing your behavior vocally as well as physically.

It's the vocal sound that is the vehicle for expression. In a variation of GIBBERISH, speak no more or less than what you're feeling using random numbers. Four, nineteen, two hundred and seven, sixty-one, etc.

Part of your job as an actor is to say words. Not your own words, but those of the playwright. You must say the words and convey truthful behavior. If, your intellect understands the line and you say the line without regard for what you're feeling when you say it, then what you are expressing is different from what you're feeling. You're lying!

By saying or expressing what you're feeling in terms of nonsensical numbers, you express and hear your own TRUTH. You are also training yourself to *create* and express truthful behavior using words. After all 'sixty-one' is a word, but you can't make any intellectual sense out of saying 'sixty-one'. So it will be expressed with whatever your truth is at the MOMENT. Part of the sensory process is to condition you to continuously express the truth.

When you watch actors on stage behaving a theatrical lie, you may understand the characters and may even understand intellectually what they're attempting to portray. You will not, however, feel it with them emotionally. You won't believe it either, and that's really a cold sensation, pardon the pun.

•Daily Activity

A sensory exercise involving the exploration and creation of a simple activity you do every day.

Brushing your teeth, washing the dishes, making the bed, and feeding the dog are just some of the choices you can use for a daily activity exercise. Daily activity is often used in combination with other sensory exercises so as to teach the actor to "think with his body", as Strasberg said.

In doing your homework for a daily activity, do the activity exclusively for your acting and not just because you have to do the activity. If you're getting dressed, just get dressed because your OBJECTIVE is to go out. When you're ready to work on your CRAFT, then take your clothes off and put them on again. This time your objective is to use the process of getting dressed to learn sense memory and work on your CRAFT. Ask all the sensory questions that are discussed elsewhere in this book under other sensory exercises.

In life you are continually bombarded by an infinite number of stimuli. When you choose COLD SENSATION or sharp TASTE, for example you are only focusing on one stimulus. When you combine those exercises with others, you teach your INSTRUMENT to respond naturally as opposed to intellectually. That is, you do what you would really do instead of doing what you think you would do.

•Drunk

A sensory exercise involving the exploration and creation of being drunk.

In order to do this one you need to have really experienced being drunk. If you never have, don't go out and drink. It does not mean that you can't play drunk on stage or in front of the camera. It just means that you won't use the actual drunk exercise to do it. You wouldn't murder someone to play a murderer.

As in the other sense memory exercises, go back to a SPECIFIC time when you were actually drunk and start asking questions relating to your senses. What position was your body in when either standing or sitting? Which muscles and muscle groups were more relaxed than usual? Also, find OBSTACLES in trying to maintain your sobriety. Remember, a real drunk is trying to appear sober. His ACTION is to appear to be sober. What physical compensation do you need to make you try to walk a straight line, or to stretch your arms out to your sides and bring your index fingers together quickly in front of your nose?

Discover what happens to your face. Do your lips feel thick? Does your jaw slacken? How much? Can you sensorily recall the way your vision was affected? Ask questions that appeal to your sense of SMELL and TASTE.

Now, should you be required to play someone who is drunk, don't automatically leap to the OBVIOUS CHOICE and create drunk. You might find that your smell exercise produced a drunk effect. If you work on sharp or sweet smell, your favorite cologne let's say, and you EXPLORE the smell for over an hour, don't be surprised if observers describe your behavior as being drunk. Sometimes SUNSHINE will create a drunk effect in actors. Some people lay in the sun and get into a sleepy drunk-like state, others may get fidgety and cranky. We're all different and stimuli will affect us all differently.

•Hot Sensation

A sense-memory exercise in which you create a specific hot sensation in your senses for playback at a later time.

In creating hot sensation or heat, first make a big CHOICE. A blast furnace would be great but may not be practical. Let's say that you will use your oven turned up to broil. You wear your overcoat, hat and gloves, you open the oven door and sit right in front of it. That's heat alright.

You can also use any variation of the hot sensation exercise such as a steam bath, sauna, or a very hot fireplace. In working on these, or on any sensory exercise, it is the HOMEWORK that teaches your instrument the responses.

Think of sense memory metaphorically as a tape recorder or a VCR. The real OBJECTS you CHOOSE to work on are what you will record. The questions that you ask and the EXPLORATION you carry out is analogous to the recording process. When you get to class and create the heat without using the actual heat stimulus, you are only playing back the original OBJECT you recorded earlier at home.

Begin the process of SENSE MEMORY by asking questions about the way in which you relate to the heat sensorily. Where in my body am I aware of the heat most? Where on my face do I feel the heat strongest? How does the heat affect my personality, my mood, my speech, and my attitude? What does the heat make me want to do?

You don't necessarily have to ask these questions in a literal way. You should try to encourage these questions to arise from your natural curiosity. Cultivate a sense of wonder. If your question is how does the heat affect my speech, you only need to speak to find an answer. If you're investigating how your heat choice affects your personality, you can explore that while relating to someone else, real or imagined.

As in other sensory exercises, the purpose is to teach your INSTRUMENT to respond to your choice when your choice isn't really there. You can train yourself to focus on SPECIFICS, deepen CONCENTRATION and build a repertoire of choices for a PREPARATION.

•Itch

A sense memory exercise involving the creation of a specific itch.

Creating an itch begins with the CHOICE of what stimulates the itch. Is it a mosquito bite, a rash, poison ivy, or something else? Once you settle on an insect bite, for instance, go back to the SPECIFIC time when you had that bite and start by asking questions (that appeal to your senses) about the itch. How do my clothes effect the itch when I move? What happens to the itch when I blow on it, stretch the skin or slap it?

One thing you don't get to do is scratch it. If your OBJECTIVE is to create an itch and you scratch it, as you might in real life, then the act of scratching begins to abate the sensation of the itch. In other words, don't scratch to alleviate an itch that you're trying to create. In real life if you have an itch your objective is to rid yourself of it, so you scratch or you treat it with medicine. In sensory your objective is to create an itch that doesn't exist.

Don't forget, as you work sensorily, to scan all of your senses from time to time. Start with your eyes if you like. Can you see the itch (a rash perhaps)? What colors are in it? What shape is it? How high does it rise from the skin? Now move on to smell. Does the smell of an ointment surprise your nose? Are there other smells? You may be irritated by an itch while someone is preparing a meal. You may associate spaghetti sauce with your itch. Now ask tactile questions. What occurs when you tickle the itch? What is its texture when you run your finger over it? When you achieve a strong itching sensation, discover what happens to you when you try to conceal the sensation—for instance, while being introduced to your new boss.

Stay in a state of wonder and question continually moving from sense to sense. The questions above are only a start, we've barely scratched the surface (pun intended).

•Mirror (shaving for men or make-up for women)

Sensory exercise using yourself as an object employing a sensorially created mirror.

This is often given second in a series of sensory exercises. Now that you have focused your attention on an OBJECT (MORNING DRINK), you can use yourself as the object with the use of the mirror. Usually men will use shaving as a physical ACTIVITY and women will use make-up to explore themselves as an object utilizing a sensorily created mirror in which to EXPLORE the physical TASKS.

First work at home for about an hour each day on all the objects that you use when either shaving or applying makeup. Explore these objects in the same manner as you would explore morning drink. Use these objects to carry out your task on your own face, using your face as a new object. Of course in the class or workshop there will be neither a real mirror nor props.

Questions you might ask of your visual sense are: How does the light affect my face in terms of shadow, line, form, and shapes? On which part of my face am I focusing my attention? My left eyebrow, my right jaw?

Tactually enjoy the textures of the tools you're using. Explore the weights of the objects in terms of how much muscle power is needed to lift them. Taste objects that you might never, ever taste. Mascara, soap, after-shave, etc. Why? So that you don't sensorily assume anything. Remember, if you tell yourself you know all about your object, you will get bored. And if you get bored, we'll get bored.

Have fun by breaking your routine. If you always begin putting on base in the same way, vary it. If you always begin shaving on the right, try something completely different. Apply lipstick to your cheek. Shave very, very slowly so that you can hear the sounds and feel the pull on each of the little beard hairs. Play with the shaving cream. Explore the texture of your various cosmetics on different parts of your face. Now work for a while without the real objects. What do your senses INSTINCTIVELY remember?

Once you begin to trust what you've created, make your ACTION to play, to wonder, to really enjoy. Avoid pantomime. It may look like pantomime to observers but pantomime strives for a representation of something real. Sensory means teaching your senses to respond to a stimulus that was real when you sense memorized it, but isn't real now. The memory of it in your senses is what's real though. The rule is simple in sensory: don't try to answer questions, just ask 'em.

•Morning Drink
Sensory exercise using your own breakfast drink as an object to explore and re-create.

This is generally the first sense memory exercise given in a series. It focuses attention on an OBJECT, in this case whatever it is that you drink in the morning or anytime for that matter. Years ago it used to be called the 'coffee cup' exercise because all actors drank coffee all the time. Nowadays, it can be anything from herbal tea, or mineral water, to Coke. The main point is that it should be sensorily interesting and stimulating.

Let's say you're using orange juice. Here's how you might begin. First, sit in a comfortable place and RELAX. Take a few deep breaths and place your glass or juice down in front of you. Just look at it.

Now you are going to ask questions that appeal to your five senses. If you ask questions that pertain to your head or your intellect, sensory learning doesn't take place. That's why some actors have a tough time with sensory work. Sense memory is nothing more that a conditioned response. It is a real response of the senses to something that isn't there. Actors get paid to create real responses to things that are not real. Okay, back to the juice.

You've got the juice in front of you. What can you ask about a glass of juice? I know all about the juice already, right? Yes. Maybe. First assume you know nothing. Pretend you came from Mars and you arrive on Earth inside a human body. You have your full intellectual capacities, but you have never before

124

experienced your senses, you didn't have senses as a Martian. It's AS IF you're seeing, hearing, tasting, smelling and touching for the very first time.

So you're looking at the juice. How far is it from your face? If you say two and one-half feet, that's a head answer. Sensorily, it's as far away as your eyes tell you it is. In other words, if you took the object away, your eyes could retain a visual image of the juice and the correct distance. Now reach out to grasp it and lift it to your mouth, or perhaps to your nose if the questions you have in mind are olfactory as opposed to gustatory (smelling instead of tasting). Break down what's happening. If you took a sip, hold it in your mouth and let your tongue ask questions about the taste. There are over 9,000 taste buds on the tongue. There are only four primary tastes. Everything we ever taste is made up of combinations of these four tastes. Where on the tongue do I taste sweet, sour, salt, and/or bitter. Is the glass a different temperature near the bottom as opposed to the top? How many muscles are involved in lifting the glass? Again, the answer isn't three muscles. It's whatever pressure in your arm it takes to lift the glass. What sound does the object make when it's flicked with your finger? What sound does the object make when it's put down on the floor, on the table, on a piece of glass?

Use your senses as you would a VCR or a tape recorder, to record the actual stimulus on one or more of the senses, and then play it back, as it were, without the actual object present. Remember, your TASK is to elicit a response from your senses when the stimulus is gone.

When you arrive at class to work on your exercise, you will have had one week of exploring the real object thoroughly. Keep in mind that it's the memory of the senses you're working for, not the actual object. I once had a student who worked on 'morning drink' and was miserable because she didn't believe it herself. When I asked her what was wrong, she complained, "I don't see it, I don't smell it, I can't taste it. Nothing." I said, "Susie, if you do see it, let me know and I'll study with you!"

Sound Advice

Now, most important. If, as you're working, you start to sense things for real; for instance, you get a flash of a smell or a genuine taste, that is an IMPULSE. Express it immediately and vocally.[1] Sound is the vehicle for expression. As you progress through the exercises week after week, they become more complex and personal. There will be more IMPULSES and therefore you will make more sounds. The sounds will be colored by what you're feeling in the MOMENT. When the sound you release expresses no more or less than what you're feeling you will be telling the TRUTH, the whole truth, and nothing but the truth. You can release the sound as a simple vocal Ahhhh! Or it can be GIBBERISH, or random numbers, or letters. It can even be your phone number, address, or the Pledge of Allegiance. Eventually you will be saying the words of the play powered by pure truthful behavior.

Sense memory is organized EXPLORATION. Avoid getting caught up in the logic of the task as you would in real life. In life we have our breakfast drink to get nourishment, fill out our routine, and wet our throats. In sensory we're using the drink to a different end. Our OBJECTIVE is to teach the senses to respond for real to a stimulus that isn't there. Our purpose is to explore, encourage discovery and vocally express what we feel in the moment.

Relax, ask questions that deal with your senses, let go, and have fun.

•Overall sensation
A sense memory exercise using a stimulus that effects the senses overall.

This SENSE MEMORY exercise involves CHOICES that use all of your senses affecting all of the nerve endings at once. Some examples of overall sensation are COLD

---

[1] So often we hear actors say they wouldn't make any vocal noises if they were drinking coffee, soaking up sunshine or tasting a lemon. We can't stress often enough, it's not as you do it in life. It's an exercise to help you believe the GIVEN CIRCUMSTANCES and express them using vocal sound. That is how the theatre audience best receives it. Emotion doesn't some from the SENSE MEMORY, it comes from your belief in the circumstances combined with a personal CHOICE of an ACTION.

SENSATION, HOT SENSATION, taking a SHOWER or bath, or inventing some fantasy TASKS such as being in a big vat of chocolate, being covered in blood, being in the rain, or swimming in a tub of Jell-O. There are infinite possibilities. You can make them up.

If you are working in a class or group that uses sense memory, your teacher or director will guide you in the progression of exercises that will best serve you and your CRAFT. If you're working on your own, start with a choice that you can actually sense memorize at home alone. You can work on cold or hot if you have access to the real stimulus. When it's cold out and heat is assigned, students are asked to find a hot spot. Maybe they put on a sweater, winter coat, scarf, hat and gloves and sit in front of a blast furnace, or an oven turned up to broil with the door open and really EXPLORE the heat.

If it's hot out and they need to work on cold, they can go to a walk-in refrigerator at a restaurant or work with frozen food or ice cubes. As you teach your instrument to respond to these stimuli you can create fantasy overall sensations, such as being covered in cotton candy, floating in a tank of spaghetti, or having oil all over your body.

The technique for doing the exercise is basically the same as in the other sensory exercises. Try to sense memorize the actual OBJECTS by asking questions that pertain to your senses and playing them back through your senses when the object isn't there. That's roughly the way it's done.

•Personal Object

A sense memory exercise involving the use of an object having some emotional significance that is sensorily re-created without using the actual object.

In the SENSE MEMORY exercise called MORNING DRINK we treat the drink as an OBJECT. In the MIRROR exercise, we use a sensorily created mirror to examine our selves and we become the object.

In the personal object exercise we use an object that has some emotional meaning for us. You might use an award you've won, a letter you've kept, a charm, or a piece of jewelry. It could be a picture,

127

photograph, newspaper clipping, or an item of clothing that was given to you by someone you love.

Whatever your CHOICE, you will use the same method as in the other sensory exercises. You will probe aspects of the object by asking questions that evoke sensory answers. That is, the answers happen in your senses when you question by *doing*. They don't happen in your head by merely thinking and not doing.

Use the whole object. If you're working with a photo in a frame, examine the frame itself, the back of it, the taste of it, the weight of it, the sounds it makes when you set it down, the feel of it against your face, your chest, and in your hands. If you find that you're limiting yourself to just the image of the photo, you cheat yourself out of so many more stimuli to respond to and express.

If you keep focused on your OBJECTIVE, which is simply to question the object in terms of your senses, you will find emotional responses that come up unexpectedly. It's as if they come around the back door and hit you in the gut when you least expect them. These emotions are the result, not the process.

When you feel something emotional happening as you work, express it vocally. Make a sound from the diaphragm. Ahhhhh! will do. Or speak in random numbers (GIBBERISH) using different numbers in place of conventional words to express what you're feeling.

Ultimately you should have a sensory MONOLOGUE to go to. A monologue that you commit to memory, just seven or eight lines of a play you will never read or work on. It doesn't matter what the material is, you just need to express words that are not your own. Should you find you're making intellectual sense of the words you're saying and the sense you're making is corrupting your own MOMENT TO MOMENT flow of behavior, return to speaking numbers or gibberish and you will be returning to the simple, elegant *TRUTH* of the moment.

Notice the contrast of your results in choosing an ordinary object, which may have been difficult to focus on at times, and making a personal choice which, by definition, will invoke very personal behavior—behavior that is exciting for audiences to watch.

•Place
A sense memory exercise involving the sensory creation of a specific place.

Working for place is the common expression heard among actors when confronted with the problem of how to make a stage set appear real to themselves and the audience. If the set is supposed to be your living room, then the audience needs to believe that from the way in which you behave in it. You will obviously behave differently in your own living room than in someone else's.

A particular place also contains numerous stimuli to which you can respond. Create for yourself your lover's bedroom and you'll feel one way. Create the school principal's office and you will feel quite another. As in any CHOICE, your choice of place should be personal. If there is no real connection to the place you're working with, PERSONALIZE your choice.

If you are working on 'place' for your acting class, then your HOMEWORK should involve a place that is accessible to you so that you can really SENSE MEMORIZE the place. Ask all the appropriate sensory questions and answer them, not in your head, but in each of your five senses. Be SPECIFIC in every aspect you sensorily record. If you're looking at a wall in your room, see one particular shelf and the books it holds. See their condition, their colors, shapes, titles, etc. What does the floor feel like under you? Is it wood, stone, or tile? Is there a rug? Does the room have a high ceiling? How does that effect your behavior? Is it a grand room that makes you feel majestic? Or is it small, untidy and makes you feel claustrophobic? What sounds do you hear, inside the room and outside? What do you smell? Your choices, as always, must be as detailed as possible.

There is a story about an actor who was praised for his role in *Billy Bud*. The captain and Billy Bud were on the deck of the ship at night. The actor playing the captain made the audience sitting in the theatre feel AS IF the ship were at sea. When asked how he did it, he said that when he looked over the rail of the deck, he didn't pretend to be on a boat or in front of an ocean. He didn't imagine a black, starry night either. He simply gazed at a specific, solitary star.

•Sharp Pain
A sense memory exercise involving the creation of a specific sharp pain.

Sharp pain is one of the SENSORY exercises we call a 'bridge' exercise. That's not an official term. We refer to it that way because it tends to be a 'bridge' between the foundation exercises like, MORNING DRINK, THE MIRROR and SUNSHINE, into the more emotion-producing sensory exercises. Strasberg usually assigned 'pain' fourth in the series, following the exercises just mentioned. Emotional sensory exercises tend to begin with sharp pain, then move onto PERSONAL OBJECT and even onto the person whom you associate with the personal object. If you can sense memorize an OBJECT, you can sense memorize a person.

In working on sharp pain, as in other sensory exercises, the goal is not to produce emotions directly. Feelings, emotions, and behavior may be the outgrowth of EXPLORING the pain, but your real goal is to explore the pain in relation to your five senses, so that your senses re-create the original pain.

In order to do that you must first choose the pain you're going to work on. It should be one you have actually experienced. This is a departure from some of the past sensory exercises in that you do not go home and sense memorize it by really causing yourself pain. You recall a real pain such as a toothache, a stomach cramp, a sprained ankle, or a broken bone, etc. For this exercise it is usually advised that you do not choose a headache. A headache is often not specific enough and sometimes such intense concentration for a prolonged period of time may produce a real headache. Let's assume you've selected a leg cramp, a charley horse in your right calf.

Start by finding the physical position you were in when you actually experienced the pain. Maybe you were sitting on one haunch to protect and keep the weight off your leg. Begin asking questions that pertain to each of your senses. If the phone rings from across the room, what happens to the way you move if you get up to answer it? Walk on it, move about and discover how much pressure your leg will stand. Jump if you dare. Even if you don't jump, what happens to you when you issue yourself the challenge? Is there a sound associated with the pain? Taste? 'Scan' the different senses if you tend to rely on only one very strong sense. Scanning the senses means asking questions that have to do with a particular sense you ordinarily might not think about.

As you work remember to control the exercise. Don't allow the exercise to control you. If you find that the pain is overtaking you and you're beginning to scream hysterically, pull back on what you've created. Rest a bit. Breathe!

While you're in the thick of the exercise, work to express what you've created through a vocal sound. "Ahhhh!" is good for a start. I don't mean to be funny, there is a sound used in acting classes to express behavior sometimes called the "acting class Ahhhh." It often sounds like what happens when the doctor sticks a tongue depressor down your throat. He asks you to say, "Ahhhh." You can speak in GIBBER-ISH and/or random numbers or letters. You can recite the Pledge of Allegiance or a SPECIFIC monologue you use for sensory work.

Usually you will work on pain or a sensory TASK for about an hour. Look for and allow variety of experience. If the pain was sharp when you actually had it, allow for it to be dull and throbbing in its recreation, if that is what is happening. Ask unconventional questions that encourage a thorough investigation. Experiment. Try transferring the pain from wherever it is, your leg, to another part of your body, your shoulder for example. See what happens. Be creative in your choices and in the expression of your responses. Remember this is not an intellectual activity, it's a sensorial one.

•Shower/Bath

An exercise that involves exploring the sensory aspects of showering or taking a bath for re-creation later.

Shower or bath is one of a series of SENSE MEMORY exercises that fits into a group called OVERALL SENSATIONS. They affect all the senses, overall.

In the shower exercise, among other things, you are dealing with the effects of different temperature changes both on behavior and the ability to re-experience the various stimuli.

To begin with, many teachers will ask that you start by slowly removing your clothes. This should be done at home, as HOMEWORK, in order to sense memorize the textures, weights of fabric, feeling of the shower steam (if there is any) on your body, and create a sense of nakedness, etc. We usually begin the exercise with the student already undressed and ready to enter the shower or bath. The reason is that our purpose is to sensorily record every aspect of the shower or bath by EXPLORING the whole experience. If you simply do what you do in life, you go on 'automatic pilot' and the sense memory doesn't happen. Rather than explore in 'real time', that is the actual time and way it takes you to wash, slow everything down. Not to work slowly for the sake of being slow, but to thoroughly investigate each MOMENT before moving on to the next. Remember you're doing this to teach your senses how to respond to what you're sensorily questioning, not to get clean.

As in the other sensory exercises, ask questions that have their answers in your senses. Questions regarding touch could be, what is the temperature in the bathroom, what is the humidity? How deep can you breathe in the steam? Where on your body do you feel cold, goose bumps, or hot and sweaty? What do you smell when you breathe in through your nose?

Visually, what do you see as you shower? Can you see vapor? Can you re-create the SPECIFIC patterns of droplets on the wall of the shower? For sound, hear not only the shower, as it sounds in your bathroom, but also the sound of your particular faucets as they turn, your feet on the tub floor (if you tap your foot on the bathtub floor), the washcloth, etc.

Since you're exploring without assuming anything, find out what the soap tastes like. Express the response vocally.

Also important, when you're in class and re-creating the washing part of the exercise, make sure your hands and sensorial soap or washcloth are about one quarter of an inch away from your clothes at all times. If you're telling your senses that you're touching wet, soapy skin, your senses won't believe it, nor record it properly, if they get contrary information, like touching dry cotton clothing.

There are times in the shower/bath exercise when we will purposely ask a student to break the sensory logic. We may ask the student to create two shower heads at each end of the shower. This is done so that when the actor decides to wash his front, he doesn't have to literally turn his back to the audience. We try to keep actors responsible and active throughout all the sensory exercises.

•Smell

A sense memory exercise involving the exploration and recreation of a specific smell.

Smell is one of our most powerful senses. We have all had the experience of smelling something familiar and instantly being transported emotionally back to another place and time. It's as if we feel the emotion before we actually remember the facts.

In my own experiments with the sense of smell, I arranged, in front of me, several smells while I was blindfolded. I used an open can of espresso coffee, nail polish remover, a partially peeled orange, and some coleslaw. Which odor do you think was the strongest? I'll tell you later, or you can perform a similar experiment. When I began my experiment I was convinced I knew which smell would be strongest. I was wrong. It was the coffee. One reason we do the sensory HOMEWORK is to never assume. Assuming is intellectual not sensorial.

Select a smell on which to work, and begin your EXPLORATION with questions that can be answered in your nose. How deep in the nose does the odor penetrate? As I move the OBJECT farther away, when do I cease to smell it? When I move the object closer to me, when do I begin to smell it? Does the smell evoke a taste? How long does the aftersmell last?

Some teachers suggest that you put the smell all around you. We ask students to create the specific source of the smell, a bottle of cologne, a flower, a gasoline can, or other.

Also, in many of the sense memory exercises actors are counseled to learn what emotions they produce. Be careful. We are not doing the exercises in order to produce emotions. The emotions are a result. As actors we do not want to go directly for results. In life we don't try to have emotions. Rather work for the simple reality of doing and believing. If you believe it and your senses believe it, play the AC-TIONS, and the feelings will come.

As you start experiencing the memory of the smell in your nose, IMPULSES will occur. Express those impulses with a vocal sound you make from your diaphragm. The sound can be, "Ahhh!", GIBBERISH, numbers, or a memorized sensory MONOLOGUE. It is the sound that takes the feeling in you and transports it to the audience.

The smell exercise isn't simply a way to train your sensory apparatus to respond to smells that don't exist. To rely solely on logic is to limit the potential uses of smell. You can use the smell exercise in other ways that may never involve the CHARACTER literally smelling anything on stage. The outcome of smell can be used for any number of PREPARATIONS. Some odors will produce anxiety, a SPECIFIC burning building for example. Other smells can make you feel in love if you're recalling your first love's perfume. What happens to you when you create the aroma of cookies baking in the oven, fresh bread, or a roasting turkey?

•Sound
A sense memory exercise involving the use of a sound to be explored and recreated.

Of the five senses, hearing is the only one that cannot be shut out. Try it next time you hear a fire engine, a persistent blue jay, a damned car alarm, or a baby crying next door. Hearing is a powerfully emotional sense. Sound moves us literally and figuratively. "Music hath charms to sooth the savage breast." Lalo Schiffrin, who has scored so many movies and television shows, says he can make you cry with a well chosen chord or two.

The most common sound actors choose for a sensory exercise is a piece of music. Other CHOICES are the ocean, ambulance sirens, rain, thunder, people talking, breakfast cooking and bad commercials. There are infinite sounds to pick from.

If you select music as your sound, make it as SPECIFIC as possible. Even the source of the music is important. Is the music live? Is it from a favorite old record? If so, hear the scratches, too. They are part of the sound. They have a stimulating effect. Use all.

As you ask questions to discover how the sound works in relation to your ears, don't try to act like you hear something. Just listen. Questions you can ask are: how much of the sound do I hear when I cover my ears? What happens to me when I turn down the volume, when I raise the volume? Is my breathing affected by the sound? Can I feel the sound vibrate in my body?

If you're listening to quieting music, allow the music to quiet you. But avoid the trap of just sitting or lying there, doing nothing. Feel exactly what you feel, but keep the exercise active. Continue to question by doing. Move around. Experiment with what you hear and express what you feel with a sound of your own.

•Sunshine

A sense memory exercise exploring the effects and recreation of sunshine on the actor.

The sunshine exercise is seemingly more passive by contrast than many of the other sensory exercises. But that is only in the physical sense.

Sunshine requires that you be thorough in your HOMEWORK, in the SPECIFICS of how you sense memorize the OBJECT (sunshine) at home. When you practice, choose a day when the sun is very bright and high in the sky. If you're assigned sunshine in the winter, don't worry, nobody said it had to be hot sunshine. Go outside and begin your EXPLORATION with questions about how the sunshine affects the different areas of your face. Where on your face do you feel the sun-

135

shine first? The forehead, the cheekbones, top of the head?

Ask yourself how you experience the sunshine through your clothing. Investigate the areas of your body that are shaded from the sun, such as your armpits, back of the knees, etc.

This is another exercise where we ask the actor to purposely break the sensory logic. We don't want the actor to use the stage lights in place of the created sunshine. He is asked to place the sun directly in front of him instead of overhead where the stage lights are.

We question actors when they become INVOLVED with the object as to what they're feeling as a result of the sunshine. However they are not to answer in a conventional narrative. They're to express what they're feeling with a sound from the diaphragm. No more or less than what they are feeling in the MOMENT. Or, they'll be asked to express themselves in detail speaking in GIBBERISH or random numbers instead of words.

The sunshine exercise can elicit many different responses. Some actors become intoxicated and drowsy. Others become impatient and even hostile in the sun.

The exercise is not done so that an actor can create real sunshine while performing in a theatre at night. It is done as part of a series of sensory exercises. It helps actors create and respond impulsively to stimuli that don't exist. You will avoid CLICHÉS and allow INSPIRATION.

Many teachers ask their students to work with their eyes closed in the sunshine exercise. It makes it easier, to be sure. This is a mistake. You should work with your eyes open. It adds more of a stimulus, and acting is done with the eyes open.

•Taste
Sensory exercise to explore and sensorially re-create taste.

Go suck a lemon! Lemon is the classic CHOICE for working on taste. Other choices might include vinegar, plain yogurt, pickles, anything sharp tasting that will provide gustatory interest.

Again, working on taste is another way to condition your taste buds to respond to stimuli that aren't there. You don't need to get caught up in holding the lemon (or other OBJECT) in your hand, because that's tactile. Concern yourself only with questions about taste and, of necessity, SMELL. Smell and taste work in tandem.

Break down the levels of taste by asking questions that appeal to each component of taste. There are four primary elements of taste. They are sour, sweet, salt, and bitter. Every taste or flavor we ever experience is made up of varying combinations of those four components. Find out in which areas of your tongue those primary tastes are located. If you focus on sucking a lemon, do you begin to salivate? That's the sensory mechanism happening, it's that simple.

•Three Pieces of Material

A sense memory exercise involving the exploration and re-creation of three different pieces of cloth.

When learning SENSE MEMORY, actors are sometimes not able to express themselves fully. They don't trust the work yet. They want 'insurance' that they'll 'get it right'. They try to preconceive what the responses 'should be'. By using a simple and unconventional CHOICE of OBJECT, the actor can avoid preconceptions of what the exercise should be and be better able to deal honestly with what it actually is.

Three pieces of material, or three fabrics as the exercise is also called, is similar to the DAILY ACTIVITY exercise in that it appears to be unremarkable andundemanding. It calls for the simple EXPLORATION of three different pieces or swatches of material. They could be wool, cotton, and silk, or fur, burlap, and nylon. Choose any three fabrics that have variety of texture, weight, and color. You don't have to cut up your clothes to do this. It's fine to use the sleeve of your silk blouse, the leg of your blue jeans, and the fur collar from your winter coat.

Begin by creating one fabric at a time and playing with it. Float it in the air. Crush it. Sense memorize its tactile sensations on your hands, face, and chest, under your shirt or blouse, etc. As in other sensory exercises, ask questions that your senses can answer. If, for instance, you're questioning the materials' taste, don't just express aloud what it tastes like by narrating it, express an instant sound reflecting whatever impulse is there.

Work from wonder and curiosity. Do unconventional things with the material. Things that come from IMPULSES as opposed to clever ideas. You can run out of clever ideas, but real creativity is infinite. It stays with you from one MOMENT to the next.

As you become acquainted with each fabric, combine them. Make sure you hear them, taste them, and smell them too. If you should suddenly feel a real sense of delight that appears to come from nowhere, that is one of many kinds of impulses that you can express vocally with a one syllable sound or GIBBERISH. As you find different vocal expressions of the impulses, include the expression of sound in the form of an author's words too. Use a sensory monologue, one where you've memorized seven or eight lines of a piece you have never and will never work on. If you find that you're making intellectual sense of the monologue or fitting it into a preconceived idea of 'how the piece should be done', change to expressing yourself with gibberish or random numbers. You will return to your own MOMENT TO MOMENT truth.

Depending on the SPECIFICS involved in your choice of fabric, emotions may accompany the exercise. If it's a side effect of the work, it is fine and wonderful. However, avoid working only for behavior. Stay with the process and whatever results will be the TRUTH. Perform the ACTION and the feelings will come.

Shakespeare, on Acting...

An hypothesis on the question: How did Shakespeare's actors play Shakespeare? Or: How I learned to stop worrying and love the Bard!

Shakespeare! The name alone conjures up a million different responses. There are and always will be Bardophiles: those who love Shakespeare's writing for the stories, the characters, and the literary value. Of all the English language playwrights known today, Shakespeare has endured and is at the top.

There are also actors who don't care for Shakespeare, although it's not often you'll hear them admit it. The latter would like to like him but find the plays they see boring. Usually they don't understand them. In one of the introductions to Shakespeare's First Folio of 1623, two actors in Shakespeare's company by the names of John Heminge and Henrie Condell wrote, ". . . and if then you doe not like him, surely you are in some manifest danger, not to understand him." So it seems that even in Shakespeare's time, his own actors knew there were people who didn't like him because they didn't understand him. I confess to have been a member of this last group.

William Shakespeare was born in April of 1564 and died on April 23, 1616. Since it isn't known precisely on what day he was born, we tend to celebrate his birthday on his deathday. We know that his later plays were performed in his second theatre called the Globe. And we have models and even replicas of the original Globe theatre sprinkled around the United States of America, where true and accurate Shakespearean productions issue forth regularly. This, despite the fact that no one really knows for certain what the Globe looked like on the inside. In fact scholars and academics have debated for centuries whether the audience faced toward or away from the sun, whether the ground level audience was sloped or not, and other details that serve the teller more than the listener.

One school says the ground level slanted towards the stage so that people in the back could see over the heads of people in front. Another school countered with the idea that if the lower level were pitched, all the water, liquid spills and urine would collect in front of the stage (they pee'd where they stood back then) and drip down into the trap door mechanisms and other secrets concealed under the stage.

Recently, after four hundred years, they found the original foundation of the Globe theatre. What did they find? The stage was in the sunlight during the performance times (about two o' clock in the afternoon). The lower level slanted towards the audience, and in front of the stage there was—a drain! Which all goes to warn, if you're not sure of your facts – make 'em up!

139

With Shakespeare it seems everyone agrees to disagree. Just look in your bookstore at all the books that continue to be written about him.

To the acting! It would be wonderful if we could go back in time to see for ourselves how Shakespeare's plays were performed. Shakespeare spent twenty years working with actors with whom he shared an intimate relationship. He and seven of these friends shared in the profits of the company and he wrote parts to be acted by them. He knew that the roles of Hamlet, Richard III, King Lear, and Othello would be played by Richard Burbage, just as he knew that many of the clown roles would be performed by Will Kempe. But did Shakespeare's company, The Lord Chamberlain's Men and later The King's Men, have the same process of mounting a show that we have today?

The first question one might ask is, how long did Shakespeare's company REHEARSE? Answer: nobody knows for sure. If you check the literature you find almost no references to rehearsal. Of course Shakespeare mentions it briefly in *A Midsummer Night's Dream*. Pyramus and Thisby talk of 'rehearsing'. But what they actually do is go over the entrances and exits. There is one document that sheds light on the subject. Henslowe's Diary has a contract listing penalties for missing rehearsals.[1] There is also a list of plays performed by the company at the Rose Playhouse,[2] managed by Philip Henslowe. Henslowe logs his company performing a different play almost every day. Within one month's time they did something like twenty-six plays, repeating perhaps two or three of them but performing those repeats at least a week apart.

How many actors do you know who've had over twenty plays in their heads at one time? Although that was their business. It doesn't seem there was much time for rehearsal. Maybe they went over the entrances and exits even the fights and the dances. Although several fight choreographers have said that they, in all probability, had a number of set routines they already knew.

Four hundred years ago there were no theatrical stage directors as we know them today. Maybe that's the

---

[1] *The Shakespearean Stage, 1574-1642*, by Andrew Gurr, (Cambridge, England: Cambridge University Press, 1980), pp. 67–68.

[2] *Documents of the Rose Playhouse*, edited by Carol Chillington Rutter (Manchester, England: Manchester University Press, 1984).

reason they did so many plays without rehearsing? So it seems the task was to prepare a show in one day, without a director and without a proper rehearsal. How might they have accomplished that? The main thing the actors had was the words. So we might conclude that the direction is in the words.

When modern actors do a play, they go home with the script and read the play several times. They know the beginning, the middle, and the end. They also know what their partners will say next. They then have to spend four weeks to rehearse it to make it look like it's happening for the first time.

In Shakespeare's time, the actors weren't given the whole play. They got SIDES, or 'part' scripts, also called 'CUE' scripts. In other words, they got their part only with their 'cue' telling them when to speak. The cue was the last three words of the actor who spoke previously. They didn't even know who that actor/CHARACTER was. Imagine acting like that. You have built in RELATIONSHIP work for one thing, because you're listening, really listening and paying full attention all the time. (STANISLAVSKI might have solved his ANTICIPATION problem if he'd arranged *The Cherry Orchard* in cue script form. But then none of the actors would be able to deal with all of the GIVEN CIRCUMSTANCES. They wouldn't know 'em!)

In the wings, or backstage[3] they referred to what was called the Platt or plot. The Platt was about three by five feet. It was posted on a peg so that the actors could read the roles they were playing, when to enter and exit, what props to take and to whom to talk. If all they had in order to prepare their parts were the words, let's take a closer look at those words.

The closest text we have to what Shakespeare actually wrote exists today in a book called Shakespeare's First Folio. There were second, third, and fourth Folios, too, but the first is considered closest to the original because it was assembled by the two actor/company members, Heminge and Condell, mentioned above.

Prior to the First Folio there were copies of the plays that were stolen and published in booklets called quartos (the large printed pages were folded in quarters for publication). These quartos were often highly inaccu-

---

[3] 'Backstage' as we think of it today was, in Elizabethan theatre, called the tyring house (or attiring house). This was literally a small 'house' or dressing room sitting UPSTAGE center.

rate (the bad quartos). Shakespeare didn't want his plays published because he made his money by being a 'sharer' in the theatre; he received a percentage of the box office and owned part of the theatre. He wanted people to buy tickets to see the plays. They had one old and trusted member of the company who kept the plays under lock and key. A 'scribe' copied the cue scripts for each actor. The cue script was hand written on pieces of paper. These papers were glued together, top to bottom, in the form of a scroll (you can see an original Platt and part of a cue script in the Dulwich College Library in England).

Pretend you're an actor in Shakespeare's time. Let's speculate as to how you PREPARE a role. The producer comes to you and says, "We plaie Julius Caesar on the morrow. Here be the role (roll?) of Brutus. Learn ye well, lest ye forget." You've just finished playing Henry the V. It's about six o'clock in the evening. Your next show is two in the afternoon the next day. What will you do? First maybe you'll read your part. What might you notice? (For a more complete discussion see VERSE TECHNIQUE)

Before you even read your part, you see the 'shape' of the piece. You might see one or two sentence lines for a while and then a bunch of MONOLOGUES and/or SOLILOQUIES. You might see some of your part written in verse and some in prose. Prose is prose, but verse is heightened language. Perhaps it is direction to act heightened behavior. I'm suggesting that the TEXT differences you discover are theatrical in nature, and not literary.

When you see a whole role unrolled, that looks as if it's been written on an airport runway, you draw different conclusions from those you would draw reading the play. The words also tell the actor his ACTIONS and OBJECTIVES. "To be, or not to be..." is also a theatrical action. It's there for the actor playing Hamlet right at the outset of his speech.

In the 'Famous Shakespeare Weekends[sm]' at Drama Project in New York, we've seen Shakespeare's staging of the vault scene revealed in *Romeo and Juliet*. The actors have only their cue scripts, no rehearsal and one simple stage direction, "cross to the person you're speaking to."[4]

---

[4] Or "cross to the person to whom you are speaking." This may not have been authentic. Who's to know? It is used for clarity. When you have a dozen actors on stage, it is the best way to let the audience know who is talking to whom.

Enter Boy and Watch:

Boy: This is the place,
           There where the Torch doth burne

Watch: The ground is bloody,
           Search about the Churchyard...

In this scene the boy knows it's dark and one cannot see (even though the actual performance is in daylight, outdoors) because he says, "There where the Torch doth burne". The Watch, who hears the boy say his line, also knows it's dark. (The Folio gives Torch a capital T. In the Folio there are many words in caps for no apparent grammatical or literary reason.)

If you ask your character to choose those capitalized words, it gives a meaning that works very well theatrically. When the Watch says, "The ground is bloody," how does he know that if it's supposed to be dark. He must kneel down to see it. He might even smell or taste the blood; after all, how would he know that it's blood? It could be water. It's great theatre because it's exciting and it's clear enough for anyone to understand. All those PHYSICAL ACTIONS are contained in the text.

Not only does the audience understand it, but the scene is BLOCKED and the stage composition is balanced perfectly with no other direction or rehearsal.

In order for this technique to work, you need to visit the library and get a hold of the First Folio.[5] That is what Shakespeare wrote. Those plays have been performance tested.

The editions that we purchase in bookstores are edited. Usually by scholars and academicians who are more interested in literature than in actually staging the plays. These editions are sold mostly to students to use in school or to people who enjoy reading Shakespeare. The editors want to make the play more understandable for the readers who are not able to see the production.

It's when editors decide that Shakespeare must

---

[5] The best facsimile is *The Norton Facsimile of the First Folio of Shakespeare*, edited by Charlton Hinman (New York: W. W. Norton and Company, Inc., 1968). As of this writing there are no facsimiles of the First Folio currently in print. If you scour the secondhand book shops you may come across a version of the Folio.

have made a mistake, or that compositor B was drunk when he set the type, or that Heminge and Condell were sloppy because they were merely actors, that they change Shakespeare's punctuation, spelling, and the words themselves. Those original, unedited words work on the stage! In fact, they work far better than the edited versions.

The best way to work on Shakespeare is by saying the text out loud. There are verse techniques that make the play and the action clear when you play them on stage. As a wordsmith, Shakespeare used many of the same techniques that advertising copywriters use today to manipulate you into buying their clients' products. Techniques like rhyming, rhythm, alliteration, assonance, metaphor, simile, sexual innuendo, oxymoron, etc. Find these 'verbal conceits'. They are the acting clues to Shakespeare's direction in the text. If you have a question, play the scene first. Then you will have your answer. The choices Shakespeare made were the ones that worked best theatrically. And that's the same for every actor today.

What you must add to the above work on Shakespeare is the basic internal work of today's actors. If you're kneeling down to check that "the ground is bloody," it helps to create the bloody ground (SENSORY) so that you and the audience believe it. There are still CIRCUMSTANCES and PREPARATIONS that need to be incorporated in order to play in a believable way the kind of large characters Shakespeare wrote. These characters were often real people who were heads of state and shapers of history. These are characters who spoke articulately with more precision and less SUBTEXT than we have in modern plays. They used words and language in a way that has all but disappeared from use today. The actor's problem is still how to do these long, witty speeches, and make them truthful so that he is creating the character who is capable of expressing the genius of William Shakespeare.

Sides

A part of a script. Usually one or two short scenes used for audition purposes.

"I've got to see my agent and pick up my sides," you will frequently hear actors say. Sometimes they are coming apart at the seams, but in these instances, both references are figurative.

Sides are just small sections or parts of a larger script. If you get a big part in a television drama, you will be given a whole script. If you have a small part, all you get are sides.

In a way sides take some pressure off you. You can only make your CHOICES on the basis of the material you've been given. You will still determine who your CHARACTER is, what he feels, what he wants, and what the does to get it. You can understand RELATIONSHIP and construct HOMEWORK for yourself before your AUDITION.

I know one major New York casting director who will say, "No, you can't have a script, but you can sit in my waiting room for as long as it takes you to read it." Why not? She wants you to get the job! If you get such an offer, take it, you'll be ahead of the game.

If you get your sides several days in advance, learn your lines. Try not to memorize them though. Learn them by absorbing them in the same way as you inadvertently learn the lyrics to your favorite song. If you've been handed sides to read cold, try to make an appointment to came back later, after you've done your homework. If you can't, develop your COLD READING skills.

Soliloquy
When a character is alone on stage and speaks, usually to the audience.

The most famous soliloquy in the English language is Hamlet's "To be, or not to be, that is the Question." Do you think Hamlet is talking to himself? According to letters and reviews in the late 1500s and early 1600s Shakespeare's company, Lord Chamberlain's Men, did some of the most realistic, TRUTHFUL and NATURAL acting around. The plays were performed in the open air (the Globe had no roof) at around 2:00 or 3:00 in the afternoon. It wouldn't be very realistic to ask the audience to believe that Hamlet was talking to himself. Not in iambic pentameter (SCANSION and VERSE TECHNIQUE). It makes much more theatrical sense for Hamlet to talk to the audience. He could see and be seen by the audience.

The soliloquy deals directly with the idea that truth in the theatre is a metaphor. Even in today's theatre, especially the smaller local and regional theatres (99 seats or less), modern playwrights are writing soliloquies where actors turn to address the audience.

It has been said that a soliloquy is the CHARACTER speaking his innermost thoughts to the audience. The problem with that definition is there are characters who speak directly to the audience and lie. Characters like Lady Macbeth, Claudius, Hamlet, and Iago often talk to the audience using language that is structured with bad jokes, puns, double entendres and sexual innuendo. It is designed to impress the audience and as such connotes an insincerity on the part of the speaker. These do not appear to be the character's innermost thoughts. They are most certainly what the character wants you to know. They are the continuation of that character's expression of who he is and what he's about, addressing the audience, with the audience becoming just one more character in the play.

If you use this premise, then you need to make the audience members SPECIFIC to you. Who are they? They could be people with whom you work. They might be a crowd of people who are supporting you in a special effort that means everything to you, or people who are against you. The audience could be your family, or just your mother. It must not, however, be allowed to remain general.

Song and Dance (exercise)
An exercise invented by Lee Strasberg that helps an actor break habits, patterns, and express impulses. In addition, a diagnostic tool for teachers.

The song and dance exercise was invented by Lee Strasberg when he was working with singers and teaching them to act. He found that singers INSTINCTIVELY put their words to the rhythm of the song. Because of this PATTERNING, or habit, IMPULSES were stifled. Habits are physicalized in the muscles. They are not bad per se. We need habits in order to live. It's the habit of inexpression that requires a method of attack. In order to 'attack' that habit and allow impulses to be expressed, Strasberg experimented with what is now the 'song and dance' exercise.

Song and dance has little to do with singing and dancing. It begins with the actor simply standing in front of the audience (the class) and just relaxing and being himself. The teacher checks the actor for RELAXATION and for impulses that come up just because he is 'on the spot'. Sometimes the impulses are so strong they will make the student fall back on one leg and throw all his ENERGY up to the lights. Other times we will just see inappropriate fidgeting, finger movements, or arm and body swaying. Often you will get an attitude that is a cover for the real behavior happening in the MOMENT. We've seen actresses who behaved coyly and actors who expressed a defensiveness. Both actors were feeling fearful of what was going on inside them.

You can see by the way an actor simply stands in PREPARATION for the exercise what might be going on within. If the feet are too close together, it may indicate that the actor will 'follow you anywhere', or a kind of military, order taking mind set. On the other hand, if the actor's feet are spread farther apart than shoulder width, it often denotes a defensive stance, or as Strasberg put it, the 'Atlas stance' bearing the weight of the world. In any case, this is but one example of how the exercise is also a diagnostic tool or X-ray into the actor's problem. It's not a normal thing simply to stand and do nothing but relax in front of a lot of people. It's the teacher's job to bring out the real behavior currently existing in the actor by asking the actor questions about what he's feeling and making constructive comments on what the teacher observes.

The next phase is the song. Here the student uses a simple song that he knows well (Happy Birthday or a nursery rhyme is common.) He does not sing, but uses the song by sustaining each note with a full commitment, one note at a time. The student takes a full breath, then releases the tone long and full. But he does not hold it so long as to loose breath. There is no acknowledgment of musical rhythm, just one note, or syllable, at a time. As the tone is released, the actor and the teacher work to allow the impulses to be expressed through the voice. A sense of the tune is strived for but is not absolutely necessary. Strasberg felt there was no such thing as being tone deaf. The inability to carry a melody was the result of early conditioning. Someone told the child that he couldn't sing and the child, not wanting to fail, began withholding musical impulses. This is part of the beginning of an inhibition of expression.

Song and Dance (exercise)

The actor should not have a preconceived idea of how to sing the song or try to 'put the song over'. What is important is that the tones not be connected in any way to the rhythm or 'beat' of the song. This not only helps to break habits, but also encourages impulses that are there to be fully expressed. During all this the teacher is assessing the actor's physical stance and both diagnosing and coaching the actor to get in touch with and release what is happening emotionally within him in the moment.

The next segment of the exercise is the 'dance'. Here the actor executes a simple movement primarily involving the torso, as the torso involves a more total body response. The actor either swings the body forward from the waist, down to the floor, or from side to side. He continues to repeat the same movement in a rhythmical manner.

While fulfilling the 'dance' part of the exercise he 'sings' the song, only this time in short bursts of sound, or explosions of sound, syllable by syllable. And he does not allow the sound to follow the rhythm of the 'dance'. The actor must commit fully to a dance movement without knowing beforehand what he will do. It's a little like the child's game of patting your head while rubbing your stomach.

The dance movements are often varied by the teacher calling, "Change!" The actor switches to another movement immediately, without any thought whatsoever. As the actor gains proficiency in the 'dance', he can 'change' himself. The actor must know enough about what he's doing to be able to repeat it exactly and accurately. Those are the demands of the theatre.

Actors need to be able to separate their vocal patterns from their body RHYTHMS. They need the ability to move quickly and talk slowly, if a director should require it, without any withholding of the actors' impulses. Song and Dance is one of the best exercises there is to help an actor break ingrained habits and fully express impulses the CRAFT allows him to create, but that an inflexible INSTRUMENT prevents him from expressing in the moment.

Strasberg said that if an actor can do Song and Dance he can do anything.

Soul

The emotional core of who you are and who the character is.
The uniqueness of you and your character.

Finding the soul of the CHARACTER means finding the character's essence. It means discovering the character's RHYTHM and uniqueness.

When we speak of people we're apt to say, "She is a 'good soul'" or "He has an 'old soul'." "I need to do some soul searching." "This food is soul satisfying!" The soul, in terms of acting, is like the bull's-eye of a target. It is what we aim for to create a fully developed character with depth and substance.

When you play a role long enough you learn more about your character than you might imagine. Your character is steadily being exposed to new stimuli and will respond accordingly depending upon how thorough your initial work on the character has been.

STANISLAVSKI continuously invoked the word 'soul' to illustrate the totality of the actor's work on his part. He used the word in a spiritual sense as well. The soul refers to the deepest most complete INVOLVEMENT and commitment one can make. It also refers to the actor himself.

Stanislavski's student, Richard Boleslavsky said, "Acting is the life of the human soul receiving its birth through art. In a creative theatre the object of the actor's CONCENTRATION is the human soul."[1]

When we experience a live performance we witness not only the performance and the CHOICES made by the actor, we 'take communion' with who the actor is. We are in the presence of the soul of that artist. And we receive the outpouring of his soul. The artist in turn receives the expression of who we are. Our souls.

We appreciate actors whose abilities and talents are on many different levels. We say, "I like him," or "She's wonderful." We may say others have more talent. They might be better actors technically, but we don't respond to them on the same level.

We respond to the essence of the artists on stage. We sense how they are living or how they have lived their lives. This extends beyond the character, beyond the performance and beyond the play. The actors are the

---

[1] *ACTING: The First Six Lessons*, by Richard Boleslavsky (New York: Theatre Arts Books, 1933).

total of their experience. This is also true of us. If we are the sum total of what we've done and what we do, we have great choices to make in what and how we take action both now and in the future.

When you know all about your character and all of your craft has been assimilated, when you are on stage thinking and behaving as your character, you might then be projecting the soul of the character to your audience. You own it. That is the ultimate to be strived for in the creation of a character, in the expression of your art.

Specifics

Focusing attention on particular details .

The more specific you are in any art form, the more TRUTH you will convey. In addition to truth, you will exact clarity and better understanding from your audience. Writers are taught to be specific in creating details to tell their stories better. Painters capture your attention with meticulous attention to specific detail. In acting too, every CHOICE you make must be specific, to you, to your CHARACTER, and to the play.

If, as has been discussed here before, you make your choices based on nature and not on theatricality, then specifics are built in. They say that in nature no two entities are exactly alike. Even things that are supposed to be duplicates are really not. There are always some small differences. The part that is different has something specific about it. The difference is specific, although we may not always recognize the specifics at the time we see the difference.

Actors sometimes think they're being specific when they're not being specific enough. A favorite teacher/director-question that actors are often asked after doing a MONOLOGUE is, "Who are you talking to?" To which the actor will reply, "My husband" or some such answer that is intended to be the right answer and satisfy the teacher or director. Now maybe the actor did SUBSTITUTE, or PERSONALIZE, or PARTICULARIZE her husband, but for a director to ask the question, "Who are you talking to?" means the choice still wasn't clear enough.

In terms of people she could choose, her husband is definitely a specific choice. But if it doesn't quite do the job, she needs to specify a bit more. Is it her husband when he is grouchy in the morning before his coffee? Is it the husband who is surprising her with an airline ticket for an unplanned vacation? Or is it the husband who has just made love to her? She is on top of him and looking down at the sweat around his tousled hair against her pillow. He catches his breath. His scent fills her nostrils, as he expresses his total love to her by asking if he can take her out to the restaurant where they fell in love twelve years ago. Maybe it's that last one. Especially if she chooses to focus on one single drop of perspiration near his hazel eye. You get the point.

To be specific is to keep asking questions. It is detail work of the highest degree. The more you EXPLORE a situation, a character, a choice or an ACTION, the more focused you will be in your doings.

At the top of this discussion we said the more specific you are the more truth you will convey. There is more. Being as specific as possible will make you believe more. In the SENSE MEMORY work, results are achieved by asking specific questions about the OBJECT you're working on. When an actor in class creates a person[1] from his life to whom he delivers a monologue, we ask him to touch the person's cheek. If there isn't a connection at that point, we ask if he has a sense of the temperature and texture of the skin. If there is still nothing we ask the actor to feel the bone structure beneath the skin. This continuous questioning and probing is really nothing more than asking the actor to be more and more specific.

Interestingly enough, the only times you need to concern yourself with specificity is when you don't have a clear idea of either the character's OBJECTIVE or your action. That may sound obvious, but there are instances when you have such an innate knowledge of your character and what your character wants, that all the specifics are already there. They come with the territory. It's only when you're not sure or you don't know, that you must consciously investigate specifics.

---

[1] A person is considered an OBJECT in sensory terms. Also the wind, COLD, HOT SENSATION and DRUNK are referred to as objects. The reason is that calling a CHOICE by its label implies a conclusion. Drunk for example implies a certain behavior that, when recalled intellectually, may spell out such a particular behavior that the actor may stop exploring and start assuming. When we say 'object' we must then investigate.

Speed-through
A rehearsal technique that involves going through the whole play very quickly.

A speed-through is a REHEARSAL that is speeded up super fast. It keeps everyone on his toes. It can show up weak spots in the way the production is shaping up and in the actors' performances. It is a variation of a LINE REHEARSAL.

Here is an extremely useful version of a speed-through for directors and for actors who are working with directors who are open to suggestions.

The actors are told to PREPARE for the speed-through at a certain point in time. They assemble in the theatre and are given these instructions: "We will do a speed-through, only I don't want anyone to speed up. What I would like is that you go through the play in normal time. But – take no PAUSES."

Some responses one is likely to hear from cast members are: "You mean even pauses that are written in by the playwright?" "NO PAUSES!" "What about pauses we've already found that work?" "NO PAUSES!" "Of course you know it will entirely throw off my entrances and exits not to mention all of your wonderful blocking." "NO PAUSES!" "Furthermore, if I should hear any of you pause, we will go back to the beginning and start the speed-through again!"

One will hear pauses. And we do go back and start again. One might have to restart this rehearsal three or four times. Guaranteed frustration. The result?

In a full-length two or three act play, you can sometimes shave off as much as forty minutes. Everything has more vitality and more energy. At the end of the completed speed-through, one can give the actors back any pauses they've earned or that are absolutely necessary. There will be some, but not many. Unless a pause is SPECIFIC to the INTENTION of the CHARACTER, it is usually not needed. If you get a chance to try this technique, you will see how beneficial it can be.

Spine
The central idea or theme of the play. The main action or driving force behind what the character wants and wants to do.

There are two spines. The spine of the play and the spine of the CHARACTER.

The spine of the play is like the trunk of a tree. The subplots and individual OBJECTIVES of the characters branch out from it. The spine of the character is directly related to the play's spine. The spine of the character was also called 'through-action' by STANISLAVSKI. The ACTION of the character throughout the play.

When an actor defines for himself the spine of the play and/or his part, it is similar to the SUPER OBJECTIVE. It is the overriding idea behind what the character wants and what the play is about.

An example from director Harold Clurman's[1] notes on the production of Clifford Odets' *Rocket to the Moon* presented by the Group Theatre at the Belasco Theatre on November 24, 1938, is as follows:

The spine of the play: To seek love (search for love).

Spine of the characters:

Stark:	To make things (his life) approximate the condition of love.
Cleo:	To seek love—the essential action of the play.
Belle Stark:	To keep her man "right," in order, safe and secure in their small world.
Mr. Prince:	He wants to find something to do.
Cooper:	To solve a problem. (If he can solve this problem he will be able to find love.)
Frenchy:	To keep going.
Wax:	To please.

Stage Business
The physical directions and the movement (spatially or with props) done on stage.

Stage business should not be confused with PHYSICAL ACTION. Whereas physical actions are CHARACTER actions ex-

---

[1] Harold Clurman *On Directing* (New York: Collier Books, 1972). Harold Clurman was an original member of The Group Theatre in the 1930s. He was cofounder of The Actors Studio along with Lee Strasberg and Cheryl Crawford in 1947. Clurman has directed some of the best known theatre in America.

pressed physically, stage business, which might include physical actions, are any precise physical stagings that the actor does on stage. For example, he crosses STAGE LEFT to the bar and pours a drink.

Recently an actor performed the opening MONOLOGUE from SHAKESPEARE'S *Richard III*. Richard begins with, "Now is the Winter of our Discontent." As he reaches the section where he comments on his deformed physicality, the lines read:

But I, that am not shap'd for sportive trickes,
Nor made to court an amorous Looking-glasse:[1]

Using Shakespeare's brilliant direction in the TEXT, the actor REHEARSED the following business. On the first line he looked at himself in an imaginary mirror, STAGE RIGHT. On the next line, he allowed the sight of his deformity to express itself in whatever physical gesture would take him away from looking in the mirror, he then said the second line back out to us (the audience). It was far more expressive and actable for the actor than to simply narrate it. In this instance the business was in the text for the actor to try. Try it yourself:

But I, (looks in imaginary mirror SR) that am not shap'd for sportive trickes, (looks away from mirror in disgust and out to audience) Nor made to court an amorous Looking-glasse:

The other aspect of stage business for students to understand is to cross out stage business in the acting editions of plays you're working on. Especially business like (she is crying) or (he enters, pauses, and sighs, and slams the books on the table). This stage business is often not written by the playwright. It is put in by the publisher to give the reader an understanding of how the production might look. Or how it was done in the Broadway or Off-Broadway production. These bits of business were discovered and tailored to the actor or star playing the part in the original production. Give yourself your due as an artist. Follow your own process. Do your own work. Make your own discoveries and CHOICES. That is how you make the part your own.

---

[1] Spellings and punctuation in the Shakespeare quotes are taken from the First Folio of William Shakespeare.

Stage Fright
Fear, anxiety, nervousness, and panic at the idea of perform-ing on stage in front of an audience.

Lord Laurence Olivier had stage fright. Many excellent and successful actors and performers, at some point in their careers, experience stage fright. It is the subject of numerous books and articles. Still it is somewhat of a mystery.

Stage fright occurs when the actor's focus is totally on himself, as opposed to his partner. But what's going on inside the actor's head? If our behavior is a product of what we tell ourselves, and in our belief in what we tell ourselves, then stage fright might be a response to a message we give to ourselves. What is the message?

Is it the so-called actor's nightmare of not remem-bering his lines or BLOCKING or even what play he's in? It goes much deeper. Fear and panic often come from the feeling of being exposed. When an actor goes on stage to behave as a CHARACTER, it implies hiding a part of himself. Even though it is necessary to 'use' as much of himself in the work as he can, there may be some small but signifi-cant part of him that fears being exposed to anyone, let alone an entire audience. To go on stage, to appear in front of an audience is to take an enormous risk.

To many actors, stage fright feels as if they're going to die. Most actors get what we might call 'normal nerves'. Stage fright is total panic. Blood pounds in your head and chest. You feel paralyzed.

In *Stage Fright,*[1] Stephen Aaron's excellent book on the subject, it is suggested that stage fright is built in to the process, that it is actually necessary.

Stephen Aaron:

> In short, I am struck by the resiliency of the actor to pressures that in others might lead to psychotic episodes. Perhaps the actor is able to control his "nightmare/daymare" precisely because he permits himself to experience

---

[1] *Stage Fright* by Stephen Aaron (Chicago: The University of Chi-cago Press, 1986). Stephen Aaron is a clinical psychologist, a director with more than eighty productions to his credit, an ac-tor, and an acting teacher at the Juilliard School.

stage fright. Indeed, we may discover that...actors are people who have to expose themselves to anxiety in order to maintain their saneness. The actor, pretending to be Julius Caesar, feels traumatic anxiety while the delusional schizophrenic, believing himself to be Caesar, does not. The actor is able to encompass the worlds of reality and fantasy by bringing them together through the medium of his performance and his capacity to return to reality may lie in his ability to solve the artistic problem of stage fright.

Actors who claim they don't get nervous on opening night are the actors you're least likely to remember. That element of risk is what the audience wants and needs to participate.

Actors can REHEARSE their lines, they can rehearse their BLOCKING, ACTIONS and OBJECTIVES. They can rehearse every detail there is, in order to minimize the risk. But they cannot rehearse the audience. The audience is the unknown. And so is the actor's fear of what the audience might find out.

Why might the audience members find out anything? They may not. But the thought the actor has in his head tells him they will learn secrets about him that the actor can't live with. All this happens in the actor's subconscious.

To create a role, an actor must tell himself certain things to affect the character's behavior. This 'telling himself' is part of 'programming' his creativity. He tells himself the character's objective. He tells himself what he must do to achieve it. He tells himself things that alter his beliefs and trigger IMPULSES. He knows he must express these impulses without editing them. Whatever comes up, he must express in the MOMENT. There's the risk. Suppose what comes up in the heat of PASSION is so personal the audience rejects him? Not the character, him! Strasberg often said, "The audience doesn't know what you're thinking. They only know that you are."

Another element of stage fright is the feeling of being out of control. Aaron talks about what happens between the time it takes from the stage manager calling,

"Places please,"[2] and the curtain going up. Even if it's only five minutes, it can seem like an eternity to the actor.

In life we use OBJECTS as coping mechanisms. We play with our keys, we twist our hair, smoke cigarettes, dust a table, straighten a picture, etc. These actions serve to dissipate nervous ENERGY. They make us feel like we have some control. When an actor is standing in 'place', his action is to wait. His PREPARATION is intense and dynamic. Where does this energy go? It goes to the stomach, the knees, the voice, almost anyplace. The result is absolute panic.

There are no easy answers as to how to get rid of stage fright. Some actors use drugs. There are certain drugs that don't alter consciousness, that is they don't get you high. They work through the circulatory system and they prevent the pounding in the head and chest often associated with stage fright. They are responsibly prescribed by physicians. Other actors indulge in superstitions. We do not advocate superstitions or drugs. We endorse education.

Stage fright has been with us for as long as individuals have had to express themselves in front of a crowd. Perhaps the answer is not to get rid of it. The answer may be how each of us uniquely learns to deal with it.

Stage Left
Stage left is from the actor's point of view.

Stage Right
Stage right is from the actor's point of view.

Stanislavski
A Russian actor/director/producer, teacher and writer. Creator of a 'system' or Method of teaching actors to act based on the principles of nature and truth in order to inspire an actor's performance.

Stanislavski was born Constantin Sergeyevich Alexeyev in Russia in 1863. The Alexeyev family members were

---

[2] In the British theatre they say, "Beginners please." That is a direct message to an actor that he is not a professional, that he has much to learn. Even though it's only a phrase, more than one fine actor has admitted being put off by it.

wealthy landholders. They made their fortune manufacturing braiding and adornments for military uniforms. Stanislavski and his eight siblings grew up learning about and loving theatre. They had on their estate a small theatre where they created plays and presentations for birthdays and holidays. Stanislavski was on the stage from the age of six. His main interest then was the opera and the circus.

As a teenager, he EXPLORED acting by dressing as his CHARACTER and going out in public to test his ability. When he was eighteen Stanislavski went to Moscow to study at the Maly Theatre, the best in Russia at the time. He began to study the actors with whom he worked. From this study he made OBSERVATIONS on what made certain actors great.

In 1882 Stanislavski went to see an Italian touring company performing SHAKESPEARE'S *Othello* starring the great Tommaso Salvini. Salvini, who was famous in part for his magnificent voice, set a new theatrical standard for Stanislavski. He was so awed by Salvini's ability to infuse his performance with such strong emotions, not only through voice but physical movement, that Stanislavski wrote it felt as if "burning lava was pouring into my heart." He also learned that Salvini would show up at the theatre three hours early for what amounted to an INSTINCTIVE PREPARATION.

When Stanislavski turned twenty-five, he changed his name from Alexeyev to that of a retired Polish actor, Stanislavski. Although it was fine to perform with his family in amateur theatre, it was not considered respectable for the manager of his father's business to be seen appearing in vaudeville and commercial theatre.

When Stanislavski's father realized his son's full passion for the stage, he funded a semiprofessional theatre for him called The Society for Art and Literature. To aid in the formation of the new company, professional playwright and director Alexander Fedotov was recruited.

Fedotov taught Stanislavski to base his characters on the observation of real people and to avoid imitation as a way of creating. Stanislavski, who was often awkward and filled with tension when he acted, developed his own ideas for RELAXATION and preparation. It was during this time that Stanislavski honed his CRAFT as an actor.

From 1890 to 1896, Stanislavski directed some of the most modern and original productions in Russia. It was only after several productions failed in 1897 that the next big change came about. Vladimir Nemirovich-Danchenko, a critic and a dramaturg from the Maly Theatre wrote to Stanislavski with the idea of forming a new theatre company. This new company would 'correct' all of the problems both men found existing in the theatres of their day. It would have at its roots acting discipline and no star system. Actors who were accepted into the company would play many kinds of parts from leading roles on one night to extras on others. It would feature innovative sets and direction. It would take chances by breaking out of the standard theatrical repertoire.

In 1898 the Moscow Art Theatre was born with the opening of Alexei Tolstoy's *Czar Fyodor*. It was a great success. Unfortunately the next few productions did not fare as well. It was at this time that the famous short story writer and humorist Anton Chekhov gave Nemirovich-Danchenko permission to stage *The Seagull*.

Under Stanislavski's direction, *The Seagull* was a hit with everyone. Everyone, that is, but Mr. Chekhov. Stanislavski had taken what Chekhov insisted was a comedy and exploited all of the commonplace behaviors of ordinary Russians. There was none of the broad OVERACTING the public was used to seeing. It felt as if there was no acting at all. It looked real. There were long pauses when characters communicated with each other emotionally, behaviorally and SUBTEXUALLY. This kind of theatre was new. It was termed 'psychological realism'. Even though Chekhov was not happy with the production, he did finally realize that the Moscow Art Theatre was the only theatre that could stage his plays successfully. The MAT became the leading proponent of theatrical realism.

The MAT continued to produce the plays of Chekhov in a realistic style. *Uncle Vanya*, *The Cherry Orchard* and *The Three Sisters* surpassed even The Seagull in popularity. The MAT did other plays, among them was Maxim Gorky's *The Lower Depths*, which created a style called 'naturalism'. The problem for Stanislavski was that, although half the plays performed were critically acclaimed, the other half were not. Stanislavski's own acting was inconsistent. There were times when he was so filled with tension that his performances fell artistically flat; so much so that Nemirovich-Danchenko actually fired him from a production of *Julius Caesar*. But there were other instances when he was inspired, relaxed, and brilliant in his acting. This internal conflict caused Stanislavski to retreat with his wife to Finland for three months to review notes he had been taking since he was in his teens. What he was looking for was INSPIRATION. He called it the 'creative state of mind'. This was in 1906. During the next six years, while directing plays like Turgenev's *A Month in the Country* and working with Gordon Craig on *Hamlet*, he began his experiments to find TRUTH in nature and encourage INSPIRATION in the work. But Stanislavski was working with actors who were already professionally trained and many of them did not embrace this new way of acting. A place separate from the MAT was needed to EXPLORE further, invent, and teach these new ideas on acting.

In 1912, Stanislavski used his own money to create and open the Moscow Art Theatre's First Studio. With the help of his close friend and assistant Leopold Sulerzhitski, classes began with the newer actors entering the Studio. Sulerzhitski, it seemed, was the only ally Stanislavski had in realizing a new and different way of training the actor. The work of the First Studio involved studies and exercises in relaxation, CONCENTRATION, AFFECTIVE MEMORY, RHYTHM, TRUTH, logic of emotion, etc. This was the beginning of what would be called the Stanislavski 'system'. The system itself was divided into two major categories, "work on one's self" and "work on the part." Work on one's self included, in addition to those exercises mentioned above, voice and diction, movement (including plastique or a fluidity in movement), dancing, fencing, acrobatics, and more. According to a chart of the system copied by Stella Adler in 1934, there were forty parts to understand on just the work on one's self. The chart is reprinted in Robert Lewis's book, *Method Or Madness?*[1]

---

[1] *Method Or Madness* by Robert Lewis (New York: Samuel French, Inc., 1958). These are the eight famous lectures given on the Method at the Playhouse Theatre in New York in 1957. At the end of the series, there is a partial transcript of a meeting between Stanislavski and the English designer Gordon Craig. They are discussing Act I, scene 3 of the MAT's production of *Hamlet* in 1909. The dialogue was taken down verbatim by Mr. Sulerzhitski.

Because Stanislavski was in the process of evolving his way of training actors, he was continuously changing things. At first he spoke of actions as objectives and then back to actions again. He spoke of the SPINE and later referred to it as the SUPER-OBJECTIVE. He did not want his system known outside the First Studio. He didn't want it written about or discussed. As leaks were inevitable, he eventually did publish his three classics on the subject, *An Actor Prepares*, *Building A Character* and *Creating A Role*.

There are many actors and creative people who disagree with Stanislavski. Or they disagree with his methods or system. But with which part of the system do they find fault? AFFECTIVE MEMORY, IMAGINATION, the long rehearsal periods, the detailed analyses outlined in Stanislavski's 'table work'? It's a good guess that if Stanislavski were alive today, he might be in agreement with those who disagree.

In the two years before his death in 1938, Stanislavski veered away from affective memory and imagination and embraced PHYSICAL ACTION as the next step in his system. In his last book, *Creating A Role*, published posthumously, he outlined twenty-five steps for directors to use in rehearsal called the Method of Physical Actions.

When you hear an artist say he is opposed to Stanislavski, ask first if he knows what Stanislavski actually said, and in what year he said it. Then determine whether the artist has any intention of infusing his art with truth, believability, and inspiration. If he answers this last question affirmatively you can smile, wish him success, and know that his quest might have gone a different route had it not been for the work of Constantin Stanislavski.

Stichomythia
Rapidly alternating lines of dialogue between two actors.

Stichomythia is one of those words one hears more in school than in the working theatre. It came from the Greek theatre. VERSE plays contained lines that quickly switched back and forth between two players usually indicating an altercation. SHAKESPEARE effectively used stichomythia in many of his comedies and histories as well.

Today it's used as a way of actually building PACE into the TEXT. Often stichomythia is meant to be over-lapped in order to create a more natural sounding situation. Some say that stichomythia includes a CHARACTER actually finishing the other character's thoughts.

The word stichomythia has a tendency to stop an actor cold if he hasn't heard it before. I personally have never heard the word stichomythia used in any theatrical situation I've ever been involved with. It does have its uses though. It has an absolute minimum value of fourteen points depending on where it's placed on a Scrabble® board.

Style
A description of the different modes of acting. Varieties of theatrical expression.

Style in life is the byproduct of actions taken by people. In theatre, it is the PHYSICAL ACTIONS taken by an actor. It is the result of what playwrights create for their CHARACTERS to do. It is the execution of a concept of ACTION by a director.

If style is a result, and we try to reach directly for it, we might be left with a veneer at best. At worst, we will have a cheap imitation of something that originally had depth and meaning.

There will always be art lovers who seek out and buy originals. And there will always be people who are content with copies. In playing melodrama (not the black and white movies of the forties but the theatrical period) for instance, we might think of a fake or perhaps exaggerated style of acting. That's not melodrama, it's bad acting. Stanislavski said that in melodrama, actors must be total in their belief of everything the playwright sets down. This is the only way the audience will believe it. If an actor doesn't believe for a moment, he will find a way to INDICATE to the audience what it's supposed to believe. The actions and the play will lack TRUTH.

When we speak of style, we might mean SHAKESPEARE or Elizabethan style, comedy, tragedy, restoration, melodrama, avant garde, theatre of the absurd, surrealistic theatre, or performance art. Sometimes you can watch an actor play a simple contemporary scene, then follow it with a scene from Shakespeare and his whole voice will change. He will speak in a manufactured idea of how Shakespeare ought to sound. It isn't real, it's his idea of style. That kind of style is not needed. The opposite of *real* is not style. Style is a measurement of the different variations in relationships. As Lee Strasberg pointed out, style is not part of expression it is a measure of expression.

If you think of how our soldiers march, and contrast it with the way that the German Army in World War II marched, you will see two different styles. If you don a German uniform of the period, you will see that because there is a tight strap diagonally crossing your torso and your boots are very heavy, it's easier to march if you move in the 'German goose-step style' that we find familiar.

During the time of the restoration, men walked in what is now called a characteristically 'foppish' walk. They didn't, I'm sure, walk that way to look like fops. They were dealing with certain realities. They were responding to different stimuli. For one thing their clothing was different. The sleeve and armholes of the period were sewn in such a way as to make it difficult to move one's upper arms too far from the torso. They had very delicate lace cuffs at the end of their sleeves that wanted protection when they extended their hands to greet someone. Their pants came down to the knees in order to better show off their calves. Calves were very sexy then. They even had prosthetic 'calves' that could be inflated and slipped under the stocking, should a gentleman have been overlooked by nature.

In the Drama Project workshops on period style, the women tie ribbons around the men's upper arms and chest to simulate the feeling of a restoration shirt and jacket. Tissues or handkerchiefs are tucked into the sleeves for the men to protect and they roll up their trouser legs to the knees. Then they parade in front of the women in the workshop. The women then vote on which male has the sexiest calves. We repeat the parade. Now the men walk differently. They walk to accentuate their calf muscles. They walk to be voted 'sexiest calves'. Now they walk as fops did because they were supplied with the same reasons that the so-called fops had to walk that way. Now they look like fops!

Style is not an imitation of a walk or a manner, it is a response to something real that must be experienced.

There really is no such thing as style from an actor's CRAFT point of view. Just the results of something real that is described to other people after the fact.

Substitution
Replacing the fictional elements of the scene with your own personal choices.

Substitution is really the granddaddy of acting techniques. It is the ultimate pretend tool. Substitution means that you replace an element of the scene that you may not believe with something real from your own life. It could be a person or an OBJECT.

In a sense, many of the terms and techniques described in this book derive from, or are variations of, substitution. PARTICULARIZATION, PERSONALIZATION, AS-IF, and even the SENSE MEMORY exercises all employ substituting something in your life for the fiction of the play.

In many descriptions and directions for applying substitution, the actor is taught to visualize or IMAGINE the person, place or thing he wants to 'use'. Often that is not SPECIFIC enough. Rather it's better for actors to 'create' sensorily, section by section, the reality they want to substitute.

If the substitution is a person, the actor can create the person's shoulders sensorily, feeling his bone structure and muscularity. One can feel or create the texture of the person's hair, the dryness or oiliness of different parts of his facial skin, his smell, and visual responses. When this basic work is created in detail, the actor can do an IMAGINARY MONOLOGUE and say to the person all of the things that he might find difficult to say if the person were really there. He can speak in GIBBERISH or random numbers if the subject matter is too private to express in front of others. It's the behavior we're interested in, not personal information.

There's a story that offers a wonderful example of substitution. An actor had to play a bad guy in a movie. In one scene he had to sneak up behind an elderly woman whom he despised and kill her by viciously striking her on the head with a lead pipe. When his colleagues saw the film, they were amazed at how real the look on his face was when he killed her. They asked him what he had 'used'.

The actor said that he went back to a time in college when he was cramming for an extremely important exam. His future was riding on its outcome. He hadn't slept in two days. It was hot in his dorm. There was one mosquito that kept on interfering with his concentration. Finally, after constant interruptions, all he wanted to do was kill that mosquito. He slowly moved away from his desk, rolled up a newspaper and stalked that insect. Quietly, he crept up to the mosquito and, with all the force he could muster, crushed the bug with the newspaper. Once this was explained to his actor friends, it became clear just how well a good CHOICE for substitution can work.

As stated in the introduction to this book, there seems to be some difference of opinion as to what some of these terms mean and how to apply them. Of all the terms listed, substitution should be the easiest to understand and use. If some part of the play or SCENE, whether an object, PLACE, or person, doesn't INVOLVE you fully, just choose something SPECIFIC from your life and substitute it for the part of the play that has less meaning to you.

It all seems so simple. But you may find that as your CRAFT and INSTRUMENT develop, and you gain more practical experience, you rely less and less on substitution. When you normally might use substitution to deal with your acting partners, you may find ways to use the other actor, not substitution.

There is a degree of INVOLVEMENT in using substitution that can take you away from the give and take with your partner. Some of your attention is on what you've created instead of on your partner in the MOMENT. One answer to this potential problem is to use your substitution in REHEARSAL only. Once you 'program' your CHOICE of substitution, let it go, trust it in performance so that all of your ENERGY will be focused on what you're doing to your partner.

Many of the techniques discussed here are like training wheels on a bicycle. They're necessary to learn balance and help you ride the bike when you don't know how. But when it's time to run a professional race they must come off. They would be in the way otherwise. There's no substitute for relying on yourself.

Subtext

The real meaning under the text. The intentions and reality behind what the character says.

Subtext literally means under the text. Webster's New Ninth Collegiate Dictionary defines it as the "implicit or metaphorical meaning" of the text.

Some say that subtext is not what is *under* the lines but what is between the lines. Subtext must be translated into ACTION or we wind up with half a play. In any case, you've noticed that people don't always say what they really mean. This is true because they often don't know what they really mean, consciously that is.

As a way of analyzing subtext, let's divide everything anyone says into two categories. Explicit and implicit. People express what they think they want you to know explicitly. Often people will tell you something that also carries with it an implicit meaning. As when a friend of yours is angry with you and, because he may not feel justified in expressing that anger explicitly to you, he tells you a seemingly unrelated anecdote that involves being angry with someone else. He gets the opportunity to express anger, even though it's not directed at you. If you suggest what really lies behind this message, he may say that it has absolutely nothing to do with you.

If you are aware of the implicit significance in peoples' statements, you can get to the meaning and feeling behind what they really may or may not want you to know.

Subtext is there to carry the TRUTH. The CHARACTER as written has thoughts and feelings, desires and wishes that are not spelled out in the TEXT. But the text is where we find the clues. Often exercises like INNER MONOLOGUE can be of help in determining the subtext of your CHARACTER. The use of OBJECTIVES and actions was STANISLAVSKI'S way of getting through to the subtext.

When Stanislavski directed *The Seagull*, it made the Moscow Art Theatre so successful that a seagull was made part of their logo. It exists to this day on the curtain of the MAT as a tribute to Chekhov for saving the theatre with his play. Everyone was happy except Mr. Chekhov. Anton Chekhov was a humorist and short story writer. When Stanislavski directed *The Seagull*, he added many things that were not written, like more than one hundred PAUSES. Not new text, *subtext*. The actors had different RHYTHMS, they held long pauses, gave long emotionally charged stares at each other, and spoke the lines in a way that made people feel as though they were seeing their own contemporary relationships exposed for the first time. This new *style* was called psychological realism. It became the MAT's trademark. That was part of Stanislavski's attempt to break away from the current state of theatrical affairs in Russia, a theatre that was filled with CLICHÉD, representational acting. This took place over one hundred years ago.

Today every actor strives to be believable. Go to a Broadway play and the most frequent audience remark you will hear about an actor's performance is that he or she was or wasn't 'convincing'.

Take the line, "It's a long time since I've had any champagne." Now take a guess as to the situation or the circumstances. What is the real meaning if the line is said by a woman in her forties meeting her ex-husband after fifteen years. How about a diehard theatre producer who has had a string of flops. The line was written, so to speak, by Chekhov. It was June of 1904 and Chekhov was gravely ill. "It's a long time since I've had any champagne" were Anton Chekhov's last words. Talk about subtext.

Super-objective
The main character objective throughout the entire play.

A CHARACTER and an actor must have at least one OBJECTIVE in each scene. All these objectives should work together toward one larger, main objective that carries the character through the play. That is what STANISLAVSKI called the super-objective.

An objective makes the actor act. In a play, there is a series of objectives. They all follow one main goal or super-objective. In choosing an ACTION to fulfill an objective, find the super-objective. It will be the SPINE of the character.

Your objective is to date the pretty actress. Your first action is to charm her. Your second action is to straighten your posture, smile, and fix your tie. Super-objective: to share your life, relieve your loneliness, be seen as loved by your friends, make love.

In selecting a super objective EXPLORE as much as possible. Some say that Hamlet's super objective is 'to get revenge'. An altogether different approach would be for Hamlet 'to seek the truth'. Those are only two possibilities that will produce two different Hamlets.

Sometimes in classes actors will experiment with many different CHOICES for actions. They may be based on the actor's IMPULSES, talents, habits, or ideas. If they don't take into account the super-objective, they wind up telling their personal stories often at the expense of the playwright.

Tasks
The individual things an actor must do to create a truthful inner and outer character.

This term began with STANISLAVSKI and Vakhtangov. They were the assignments that needed to be completed in order to create the inner and outer CHARACTER. They included finding and working with, the appropriate ACTIONS, OBJECTIVES and GIVEN CIRCUMSTANCES of the play.

As in other 'system' and METHOD terms, the word task is used today more loosely to describe almost anything that an actor must do, including simple STAGE BUSINESS as well as psychological ADJUSTMENTS.

Tempo
A rhythm that is outside of the character, coming from the environment. Its current use is slow, medium, or fast. Timing.

Originally 'tempo' was used by STANISLAVSKI and Vakhtangov to indicate a RHYTHM that existed outside the CHARACTER. If you are in a busy airport and you haven't bought your ticket yet and you hear an announcement that your plane is now boarding, your personal timing changes. There is a new tempo that comes from the airport and the situation, as that stimulus affects you.

Tempo is an extremely limited form of rhythm. It is, in a way, like timing or PACE. A difference in tempo can spell the difference in meaning. Playwright Jeffrey Sweet, in his playwriting workshops for Drama Project in New York, offers the following examples:

Example one:

She: Do you love me?
He: (abruptly) Yes.

Example two:

She: Do you love me?
He: (long pause) Yes.

Most people in theatre today aren't referring to the original Stanislavski meaning when they speak of tempo. They generally mean faster or slower or somewhere in between. Think about the origins of tempo the next time your director uses the term in his NOTES to you.

Text Analysis
The systematic examination of elements in the script in order to understand and play your part.

Text analysis is a way of understanding the script so that you play what the author intended and find clues that will enable you to act the part to your best ability. To do this proficiently, you need to know the play's THEME and you should understand the ACTION of the play and of your CHARACTER.

When you first read a play you are in the position of the audience in that you are experiencing the play's surprises in the way the author intended. At least that's what the author hopes.

The second and third times you read the play you begin your analysis. You start discovering elements and nuances you overlooked in the first reading. You also find answers to questions raised in your initial reading. Each time you read the play (you will read the play many times as part of a thorough PREPARATION) you turn up more clues about your character, RELATIONSHIPS with other characters, and your circumstances.

Of all the ways of analyzing text, theme may be the most important. The theme is what the author is saying through the words in the play. It is why he or she wrote the play. It is the heart of what the author needs to communicate the ideas in the play.

Theme is often the hardest part of a play to uncover. The reason? In a well constructed play, the playwright will state the premise and leave the conclusions to the audience. That is, the playwright will invite the audience's participation in experiencing and grasping the play. Information needed to access the play is skillfully and gradually revealed during the course of the play in a way that encourages the audience to become involved. If for instance the playwright tells you that $5+2=7$, the audience says, "yeah, so what?". But if the playwright says $5+X=7$, the audience immediately and involuntarily fills in the X. Bingo! Full audience participation!

Also, characters often say one thing and mean another (SUBTEXT). Stage directions, printed STAGE BUSINESS, scenic design, sound effects and costumes also help tell the story.

Since your job is to create the role and play the character's action, it becomes crucial to understand those actions throughout the play. Through your understanding of how the action is plotted, you can make CHOICES that lead you to fulfill your character's OBJECTIVES. You can break down the play in terms of action by creating a kind of 'action map.' When you know what your character is doing, you know what you are doing.

Good text analysis requires experience. The more you do it the better you get. This is where it is helpful to understand and master TEXT TECHNIQUE.

EXERCISE
Romeo and Juliet is about...

1. Teenage suicide?
2. Family feuds?
3. Planned marriages?
4. Unplanned marriages?
5. Three hours?

Text Technique

A systemic approach to finding the logic, meaning, and theatrical direction in the words. A direct line into the playwright's head.

It is the words themselves that urge our IMAGINATION toward CHOICES we make to stimulate behavior for theatrical expression. Both meaning and a sense of CHARACTER begin to emerge just from a grouping of words. A playwright or screenwriter creates a script by writing draft after draft, adding and subtracting words until he reaches his desired results. As actors we can learn a lot about what choices to make based not just on what the words mean, but on the power of the words themselves.

Words contain their own power. There are four letter 'curse' words that, by their very nature, will produce maximum discomfort. Some words support a loud, strong voice, "HELP!" Other words are so strong that to say them loudly with strength reduces the power and the meaning of the word. If I shout "YOU'RE STUPID!" you'll probably think that I'm really the stupid one and not pay me much mind. However if I say to you in a quiet relaxed way "You are *stupid*," you then might get pretty angry at me. In the first instance, I'm putting more power on the word than the word will hold, thereby diminishing its natural power. In the second example I'm not adding power to the word, but simply releasing the word's own power.

Often when we are in a heightened state of emotion, we will speak in a more poetic or articulate manner. When a person suffers the loss of a loved one he will usually say very few words. He may say "Oh, God," or "My Lord," or "Jesus Christ." But a few days later at the funeral, he will speak extemporaneously, elegantly, and from the heart. His thoughts and feelings will emerge easily from his subconscious into unrehearsed words. It's the same with writers.

If we use these OBSERVATIONS as acting notes we are in a better position to make choices that tell the story of the play as opposed to our own personal story, which may or may not parallel the play.

How?

It's been said that when a playwright writes a play he's also directed it. As actors we can find that direction in the text and begin our EXPLORATION from that point. That

171

is, we can make our choices armed with the playwright's intended direction.

For purposes of understanding text technique, let's look at two different kinds of lines that a playwright writes. In any play, a writer will write a line that is either simple or complex. Using that simple observation we can detect direction in the text.

If a line is simple say it *simply*. But if the line is complex, you need to choose the parts that complicate the line. The 'parts' that can complicate a line of text may be an obscure word, a rhyme, some alliteration or assonance, or possibly sexual innuendo. There might be a word that is purposely repeated. When you find these 'clues' ask your character to choose the complicating words, to do something theatrically with those words or phrases that complicate the lines. Choose the complicating factors.

How many times have you heard Lincoln's Gettysburg Address, particularly the ending? It goes: "...that we here highly resolve that these dead shall not have died in vain. That this nation, under God, shall have the true burden of freedom. And that government, of the people, by the people, and for the people, shall not perish from the earth."

Readers of that speech always emphasize the words **of**, **by**, and **for** when they perform the speech. In this technique, the clue is that the word 'people' is repeated three times. What do you do? Choose the word 'people' and build on it. Try saying it out loud this way. Imagine how Lincoln must have been received by the crowd: "government, of the *people*, by the *people*, and for the *PEOPLE*, shall not perish from the earth." After all, Lincoln is talking to people about people, not prepositions. After telling this story in class, an older woman raised her hand saying that her baby sitter's grandmother heard Lincoln deliver the Gettysburg Address and that was exactly the way he had delivered it. It makes sense. You can feel the power of the statement. It's much more theatrical.

Look at some text clues in a monologue from William Snyder's *The Days and Nights of Beebee Fenstermaker*. Let's take only the first part:

BEEBEE: I guess so. I had to get out, though. My family life was very complicated. It's funny.

On the one hand I believe my future's as bright as a button and nothin' can stand in my way. But sometimes when I'm home, a little devil gets next to me and says, "Beebee, you fly mighty high in your own mind's eye, honey. But if you ever took the trouble to look two inches past your nose you'd see your life was signed, sealed and delivered before you were born. And it's got nothin' to do with love or careers or flights of fancy." They talk about what they're gonna do or what they should have done but they're just sittin there waitin for the axe to fall....

In order to get a feel for this text technique, let's go over some text choices one line at a time.

Line 1: "I guess so." Ask yourself, is it simple or complicated? It's as simple as it gets.

Line 2: "I had to get out, though." Still simple, but notice that there are twice as many syllables. Something may be beginning to slow you down.

Line 3: "My family life was very compli-cated." It's still simple dialogue. But can you see that it has jumped to twelve syllables. Now in this technique you don't have to count syllables or words. Just notice that each of the three lines is progressively getting longer. Say them out loud. Allow the last line (line 3) to slow you down.

Line 4: "It's funny." That's so simple that it forms a stark contrast with the previous line. Get your character to use that idea. Do something theatrical with it.

Line 5: "On the one hand I believe my future's as bright as a button and nothin' can stand in my way." Contrast this with the last. It's really long. Choose to say the word 'button' because you like the way it alliterates with the word 'bright'. Choose 'nothin' because it assonates with 'button'. Do you hear the "uh" sound in both the words? Choose them.

Line 6:   "But sometimes when I'm home, a little devil gets next to me and says, "Beebee, you fly mighty high in your own mind's eye, honey." First you have a quote which indicates a GEAR CHANGE, it's your choice, just do something different. Maybe it's a change in rhythm. Look at the phrase, "a little devil gets next to me", Can you spot the assonance? It's "Devil, gets, and next." Give yourself a good acting reason to choose and use the build on "devil, gets, and next." Listen, when you say it aloud, eh, eh, eh. Now here comes that quote. What do you notice? More assonance. You have five 'I' sounds to enjoy. "Fly, mighty, high, mind's, eye." Aye, aye, aye, make it fun. See where the words lead you. Forget for a moment what the words mean. Leave yourself wide open for the playwright's intentions to enter you. Let the 'I' sound change the shape of your face. If you say 'I' or 'eye', look at what happens physically to your mouth and face when you exaggerate it a bit. It's almost reminiscent of Michael Chekhov's PSYCHOLOGICAL GESTURE, though let's not confuse techniques.

Line 7:   "But if you ever took the trouble to

> look two inches past your nose
> you'd see your life was signed,
> sealed and delivered before you
> were born." Alliteration in "took,
> trouble, to, and two" also "But, be-
> fore and born". There is also what
> we call a 'list'. "signed, sealed and
> delivered" is a list. You need to be
> careful about lifting your voice on
> the comma's and then dropping
> your voice on the period. It's also
> however, a CLICHÉ, which is a NOTE to
> say it as a cliché.

Now with all this pointing out of alliteration and as-sonance, it must be emphasized that you can't play an al-literation or an assonance. These are merely clues for you to make text choices. When you find the clue, it means you ask your character to do something theatrical with the choice. Don't say it because it rhymes, say it be-cause you're playing the character who wants and needs to make a rhyme in that particular place in order to com-municate who she is and what she wants to do.

When I say, "Ask your character to choose," I don't necessarily mean to emphasize it, or say it louder, al-though those are ways of choosing. You might say it softer or you might put a PAUSE before it or after it. You could slow it down or speed it up. Any of these choices will let the audience know your character is making a choice.

When you become familiar with this skill, you will find that the choices create an attitude in you. It's that attitude that begins to define your character.

This text technique is analogous to laying down the tracks of a train. It's technical, and in and of itself, it doesn't go anywhere. But when you do the internal work and get your 'engine' going, you will find that all of your 'locomotive' power can be fully released because you can rely on the 'tracks'. The two techniques work to-gether to take you where you want to go in record time.

Using this approach works beautifully, except in the case of some translations. It will work in some transla-tions, depending upon the artistry of the translator. Re-cently we did a demonstration with an actor who re-turned to class after a two-year absence. She knew how to create TRUTHFUL behavior, but the text work was new to her. After doing her MONOLOGUE INTERNALLY, creating very affecting behavior, she then repeated it using only the text choices that we found. She did not employ the internal, behavioral work. The audience actually preferred the latter. There was less emotion from the actor, but the audience understood more of the piece, which in turn allowed it to feel more of what she was feeling in the first go around.

 In using this approach, you will insure that you rise to the magnitude of the character and not pull the character down to your level. We are all trained to make our choices based upon the situation. Now you can make choices based upon the text as well.

Theatre in the Round
A theatre, indoors or out, that has the audience surrounding all four sides of the stage.

Theatre in the round is really what ARENA STAGE is meant to be. That is, arena used to be and technically is theatre in the round.

 Certain plays can be staged very effectively in the round. Care must be taken though. If you lose the audience for a second, it's apt to watch the rest of the audience on the other side of the stage. After all, if you don't believe what's happening on the stage, you *will* believe the guy on the other side in the audience picking his nose.

 As in arena stage acting, actors and directors need to be aware of BLOCKING. If an actor is center stage then he or she will, of necessity, be cutting out fifty percent of the audience's view. Should a scene demand almost full view, the actor should be staged near the edge so that over ninety percent of the audience will see her.

Theme
The playwright's statement through the text of the play. What the author wants you to know.

Theme is really a playwriting term. But it is an element of which actors need to be cognizant in order to make CHOICES that tell the playwright's story and not just the personal story of the actor.

In music when we hear a recurring melody through-out the piece, we say that this section of melody is the theme. It is what characterizes this particular piece of music. It's the heart of the composition.

A play is like a musical score. When all the elements of a play come together there is the intelligence of the play or, the 'head'. And there is the feeling we take away that is related to why the playwright chose to express these ideas and emotions in this story in play form: the 'heart' of the matter, the theme.

As an actor part of your choice selection in PREPARING a role must take into account the theme. How do you play theme? Of course, the answer is you can't.

This is one of the most difficult concepts to teach new actors. The way we do it in our classes and work-shops at Drama Project is to deal with the TEXT. There are many SPECIFIC clues in the text. Words are the only actual tools with which the playwright can create the story. As you learn to choose certain words for the same reason the writer chose them (because this is the way the au-thor wanted to create the character) we have a synthesis of both the author's and the actor's choices. Out of this the theme emerges. One of the difficulties with defining theme is that theme is interpretive, and there are fre-quently more than one in a good play. To paraphrase Boleslavsky, rather than ask what the theme is, it is more useful to understand how the theme perseveres through all the OBSTACLES in the play.

Thrust Stage
A stage permitting the audience to sit on all three sides. Similar to an arena stage.

A thrust stage is like an arena stage except that the stage extends much farther out into the audience. When ones think of an arena stage, one thinks of a stage that is semi-circular. The audience sits around it on three sides.

With a thrust, the stage extends out from a house wall or barrier where no audience can be seated. The other three sides have an audience; two of the three sides are extremely long and one is relatively short. The ultimate thrust stage is in Atlantic City, New Jersey. It is the Steel Pier and it is where the Miss America Pageant is held annually.

Transition

The technical switch from the end of one beat to the beginning of the next.

Webster's says a transition is, "a passage from one state, stage or place to another. A movement, development, or evolution from one form, stage, or style to another."

METHOD actors who talk about BEATS, INTENTIONS, ACTIONS and OBJECTIVES will at some point speak of transitions. Whether an action is accomplished or not, a new one will soon takes its place. That gray area between actions must be acknowledged and specified. That is the transition.

Often actors will mark transitions in their scripts. In a sense they're like milestones in the journey of the SCENE or play. They mark the spot where attention must be paid to what to do next. Example: I want to scare and intimidate you in order to get you to sign a contract. You give in and sign. Transition. Now I want to apologize and calm you.

You will sometimes hear an actor say to a director or teacher, "I don't understand this transition. How do I get from here to there?" Sometimes a CHARACTER seems to be talking, and seemingly out of nowhere he starts to cry. Finding the transition means finding the stimulus or the cause that creates the change in the character's and the actor's behavior. The actor who finds the right transition is the actor who will make us feel and understand the ORGANIC reason for the actions we're witnessing.

Truth

The expression of actions that are essentially true.

Every actor, every director, every school, class, and book on acting will tell you to "play it for truth." It sounds so obvious. If everyone out there is determined to be truthful, real, genuine, etc., why aren't all actors great and/or famous? Perhaps it's the actors perception of what truth is.

There is the Rashomon concept of several views of one basic fact. That is, I saw it one way, you saw it another, yet we're both telling what we believe to be the truth. But that truth is a perception or view of a fact. The fact is constant. It doesn't change.

When we see Superman fly in the movies we don't really think he can fly, but we accept a certain metaphorical truth within the GIVEN CIRCUMSTANCES of the story. Conversely, if Superman were to sexually harass Lois Lane, we could believe the actor playing Superman was capable of the action (more so that than flying) but we wouldn't really believe it in the context of the theatrical metaphor.

What we're really striving for is the essence of truth. When an actress slaps an actor on stage, we know it's a stage slap but we react to the essence of the truth. In fact, if the truth is too real and we think the actor really got hurt, we come out of the play because we're less concerned with the truth and more caught up in the fact that one actor lost control and another got hurt.

Theatre is a metaphor. Whatever is presented to us on the stage is an essence of the truth. No matter what takes place on stage, we know that we are in a theatre and the actors are saying lines in a play that's been REHEARSED and directed. That sounds obvious, but there are new actors who continuously strive to be real, believing that, if they are, they will attain theatrical truth.

Theatrical truth exists in naturalistic plays, VERSE plays, musicals, slapstick comedies, etc. When you are playing a NATURALISTIC scene, realize that there's a difference between being real and being truthful.

Type
The categorizing of actors, by appearance, according to the roles in which they are apt to be cast.

The important question here is: Do you know what type you are? And if you do, what type are you? If your answer is, "I'm an actor. I can play anything!" then you need to take a harder look at the business. Type casting is often a bitter pill for actors to swallow. If you are a large, ruggedly handsome man with chiseled features, then you're not going to be 'right' for Willy Loman in *Death of a Salesman*. Sure you could do a brilliant job playing it, but you're not right for the part.

STANISLAVSKI spoke about casting the SOUL of the actor for the CHARACTER as opposed to the EXTERNAL part of the actor. That is the ideal. In the current state of show business that is not likely to happen. Yes, there are exceptions. But they are just that, exceptions.

179

If there is something unique about your physicality, either fix it or use it. If you feel that you honestly need a smaller or a straighter nose, smaller or larger breasts, or hair transplant plugs, then get some honest advice, and if you still feel you need to, get it done. But you don't have to. If your nose is large, 'use' your large nose in your work. Put some of the focus of your CHOICE into your nose. No matter how still you keep your head, we'll still see your big nose. Accept it. It's you. If you take responsibility for it, everyone else can relax about it too.

If you're overweight and you get cast in a play, realize that your first NOTE from the director is that your weight is exactly what's needed. Use it. Understand why you were cast and create the CHARACTER who has the physicality you have.

A few years ago a student was referred to us by the Ford Talent Group, the talent division of Ford Models. She was a wonderful actor, however she hated modeling. She began to gain a lot of weight in order to "have to stop work." Ford's response was to put her in its large size division and keep her working. She called me to coach her for a film audition she had. I worked with her three times, and she was doing wonderfully. She also lost weight and was back to her original size. She asked me if I thought she had a chance to get this part. I explained that her work was excellent, but the part called for her to be the fat best friend of the lead. Her answer was one I'll never forget. She smiled and said, "Oh don't worry about that. I have professional fat padding that I use for work." She was still in the large size division of Ford. She knew exactly what her type was and could be. It didn't bother her in the least to be fat if it was for a job.

If there is some part of you with which you're not comfortable, find out how you may be subconsciously overcompensating for it. Casting directors, agents, and directors pick this up quickly. If you're a man who is not as tall as you would like, don't compensate by acting with a deeper voice than you normally use. If you're a very tall woman, stand tall and express your full power.

There is something very uplifting about seeing an actor audition or perform who knows himself. Drama Project once received a picture and résumé from an actress who looked nice enough. Under the picture was a second shot of her smiling. Each of her teeth had a small space between them. It looked very funny and she knew it. We will never forget her. She is saying that if this is what you need, I've got it and I know how to use it. Brava!

We also see many more actors who don't know what type they are. They are the ones who ask directors, agents, teachers, casting directors, anyone. And they keep on asking because they are not able to accept how others see them. Find out your type and sell your type. In a casting office, the last file you want your picture in is the one marked 'versatile'. It's the last place anyone's going to look.

Up Stage
The part of a proscenium stage that is farthest from the audience. Also, physically stealing a scene from another actor.

There was a time when stages were literally pitched at an angle so that audiences could see better. Up stage was actually at the top of the 'hill' nearest the scenery. Actually, it's still done for many productions. See DOWN STAGE.

Up stage also refers to an actor moving up stage so as to force his or her partner to turn his or her back to the audience. If someone does that to you, you're being upstaged. Who says you have to turn around to look at your partner? If you inadvertently do it to someone else, sneak back down stage. Get in the habit of acting to make your partner look better. When the SCENE works, so will you.

Verse Technique
Finding clues in the verse to uncover the direction in the text.

There are countless actors who tense up when they're confronted with text written in the form of verse. *Who talks this way?* they wonder. They see it as a violation of their inherent 'truth sense'. What's really unfortunate is that they just don't do verse plays. They simply avoid the problem. Can you imagine what some of the actors we admire today could do for the theatre if they expanded their talent by learning some simple techniques that would enable them to act the works of geniuses?

The Premise

In the section on SHAKESPEARE, there are some conclusions on which we can draw to form the basis of this verse technique. This way of EXPLORING verse is based in part on a book by Richard Flatter called *Shakespeare's Producing Hand.*[1] Dr. Flatter translated Shakespeare's plays from English to German. As he observed differences in the many editions of the plays available, he decided to return to the originals of the plays themselves, the First Folio of Shakespeare published in 1623. What he found in the original, unedited text, were different spellings, line divisions, and punctuation previously thought to be mistakes that might actually have functioned as Shakespeare's hidden direction to the actors. The refinements of this observation have been and are being utilized with excellent results through the work of Patrick Tucker's Original Shakespeare Company, Ltd. in London. The OSC examines how Shakespeare's actors might have acted their plays four hundred years ago.

In the entry on Shakespeare we established that during his time there were no stage directors as we know

---

[1] *Shakespeare's Producing Hand* by Richard Flatter (New York: W. W. Norton & Company, Inc., 1948).

them and virtually no REHEARSAL. How they might have accomplished a different play every day and a brand new play just about every two weeks with no directors and no rehearsals is what this approach to verse should answer.

When you read a Shakespeare play, you're reading a play that was never written with the intention that anyone read it. Shakespeare did not want his plays published. He wanted them performed. These plays were not literary endeavors, they were theatrical projects, blueprints, if you will. They were written only for the actors to play aloud on the stage.

Shakespeare's interest was in making money. The written plays were the wealth of the company. As Shakespeare was a 'sharer', that is he earned a percentage of the box office and was part owner of the theatre as well, he and the company needed protection from those who might steal the plays and publish them. These pirated plays were printed in quarto form, and because they were inaccurate, were labeled 'bad' quartos. About half of Shakespeare's thirty-seven plays were stolen. When this occurred the company would issue an accurate or 'good' quarto.

It's interesting to note that when there were no bad quartos, there were no quartos published at all. When the First Folio was published seven years after Shakespeare's death, seventeen of the plays saw print for the very first time.

Partly as a safety measure but mostly for expedience (photocopying was several centuries away), actors were not given copies of the whole play. Doing a different play every day, a scribe would have fifteen or sixteen whole plays to write out in long hand daily. The actors were given only their parts.

The 'Cue' Scripts

The scripts given to the actors were in the form of 'part scripts' or 'CUE scripts', because they contained only one's parts and his cue's. Each actor saw sections of text preceded by a two- or three-word cue. The cue was spoken by whomever it was who spoke before he did (that's right, the actor didn't even know which character was talking before he spoke). The part pages were pasted together and rolled up on a scroll. The only cue script still in existence is in the Dulwich Library in En-

183

gland.[2] In our Shakespeare Workshops in New York, actors play scenes with cue script scrolls and without rehearsal. It always works because actors find them easier to play and audiences understand and experience the play more completely.

When the actors are given cue scripts on scrolls, they instinctively roll them inside out, with the writing on the outside. In this way they can read the whole part without opening the scroll, using both hands in the conventional fashion. All they have do is hold the scroll in one hand and secure the other end with some string or a rubber band, and they can roll it. It now functions like a little teleprompter. The actor can hold it in one hand down near his waist and discretely glance down at it when necessary.

So four hundred years ago an actor was handed his 'role' for the next day. What did he see? How might he have gone about PREPARING his part? He didn't really know the details, what the play was about.[3] And if there were no directors, where did direction come from, if indeed there was any direction at all? Direction could come from one place only, the text itself.

Why Verse and Wherefore Prose?

When the actor opened the roll he made certain observations that modern actors cannot make (unless they are doing summer stock and using SIDES). He saw some sections written in prose and some written in verse. He would recognize the prose sections immediately on sight. The sentences ran into each other, as in the paragraph you're reading now. But see the difference:

> He saw verse in sharp contrast to the prose, just by
> looking.
> He knew it because the first letter of each line was
> capitalized.
> He knew that this was a heightened form of lan-
> guage.

---

[2] The cue script in the Dulwich Library is the part of Orlando in *Orlando Furioso* by Robert Greene and played by Edward Alleyn. Alleyn was the founder of Dulwich College.

[3] The principal actors in the company, as for instance Richard Burbage, would have the play read to them, but they still had to have a way to find specific moments in the play, to work on details.

He may also have presumed that, at that point in
the play, his character
Was in a heightened state of emotion.

He could also see the 'arc' of the CHARACTER: the AC-
TION and behavior of his character from the beginning to
the end of the play. He might discover for instance that
he had few lines here and there in act one, the same in
act two, but in act three he had four long speeches. In
those long speeches there might be some long passages
in verse and a couple of lines of prose, then back to
verse for awhile. He could see that there was obviously
something going on in those two prose lines. He could
find clues. He could find a lot of clues considering he
hadn't even read his part yet. He had to work fast. He
only had a day!

There are no special guidelines for playing the
prose other than some common sense TEXT TECHNIQUES.[4]
The directorial note might be: since it is written conventionally, or in a straight forward manner, the actor
should play it in a straight forward manner.

Verse is something else again. If you speak a section of verse out loud, listen to what happens with your
stresses.

Mary had a little <u>lamb</u>.
His fleece was white as <u>snow</u>.
And everywhere that Mary <u>went</u>,
The lamb was sure to <u>go</u>.

The meter of the verse leads you to give the last
word of each line a stress, or better put, a 'choice'. If
you've ever tried to construct verse yourself, you know it
isn't easy. Couldn't Shakespeare have saved a lot of time
if he simply wrote in prose? By writing certain passages
in verse, he could 'direct' an actor to stress or emphasize the last word in a line. He could choose any word he
liked to be last. This would give a particular meaning to
the line. The actor can use the verse to help him act the
part quickly and accurately. He will not try to 'smooth

---

[4] The text technique is my extrapolation of Shakespeare verse
technique. As you experiment with these techniques, you will
find your own ways of interpreting the clues in the text.

out' the verse to make it sound and play like prose. Obviously, if Shakespeare had wanted prose, he'd have written it.

Verse also has a rhythm, a cadence that makes it easier to learn. Shakespeare mostly wrote in a pattern of rhythm called iambic pentameter. An iamb, or iambus if you prefer, is a unit of measurement used in analyzing poetry. There are trochees, anapests, dactyls, spondees, etc. An iamb is two syllables. The first syllable isn't stressed and the second syllable is. For example, the words denounce, proclaim, technique, compose, and between are all iambic. De-**dum**. Put five iambs in one line of verse and you have *iambic pentameter*. Or more simply, five sets of de-**dum's**. Analyzing verse this way is called SCANSION. In verse plays like Shakespeare's, teachers and directors often want actors to know how to *scan* the lines. What directors really want is for you to know how to use the verse to be brilliant in your part. They think scansion is the only means to that end. You can read over the section on scansion and get out your Shakespeare plays to try it, if you like, or you can simply count to ten.

> De-dum, de-dum, de-dum, de-dum, de-**dum**,
> De-dum, de-dum, de-dum, de-dum, de-**dum**.

Say it out loud, see how it feels. If you feel silly then try:

> – / – / –   / – / – /
> Is this the face that launched a thousand ships?

Actually, that does have more class than de-dum, de-dum, etc. Can you feel the rhythm? Try this: you and a friend talk about who gets the last slice of pizza. Only do the IMPROVISATION in iambic pentameter. See what happens.

> Him: That slice is mine, you know, because I paid.
> You: It's just like you to throw that up to me.
> Him: If you would buy a pie yourself sometime...
> You: I hate to hear you keep up with that whine.

Now, you don't need to scan the lines, just count 'em up. Use de-dum's and your fingers if you need to. What do you notice? First of all, it takes time to think them up. If you play the above game in front of other people, and you come up with a clever line, the people give you a resounding, supportive response. What happens to you? You register pride. You express pride in your face; your body may even do a little dance or you may just look smugly at your partner. The point is, when you experience the feeling behind shaping a character's words and thoughts into a particular rhythm, you will pick up an attitude. That attitude will define your character. The metric feet, scansion, rhythm, etc. is only one part of it. There is, of course the choice of words or content of the line.

Is It Simple or Complicated?

Is the first line you say simple or complex? If the line is simple say it simply. If, on the other hand, the line is complicated, you might conclude that this was Shakespeare's way of saying, play it 'complicated'. You do it by finding the components that complicate the line. Then ask your character to choose the complicated parts. That means you do something theatrical with the word or the 'verbal conceit' that is the complicating factor.

> To be, or not to be, that is the Question:
> [Simple - say it simply]
> Whether 'tis Nobler in the minde to suffer
> [Getting complicated]
> The Slings and Arrowes of outragious Fortune,
> [Complex. Choose the metaphor]

Verbal Conceits

What complicates a line of verse? There are many complicating factors. Rhyme, alliteration, assonance (when the vowel sounds sound alike), double entendres, speaking in metaphors and similes, puns, a play on words, sexual innuendo and others. These complicating factors are called 'verbal conceits'. They work like this.

If you have two lines of text that obviously rhyme, the note is to play the CHARACTER who wants to make that **rhyme**.

Suppose, for instance, you notice **alliteration** (several, same sounding consonants) in your first section of verse. Let's say you see two or more words beginning with the letter 'S'. Choose to do something theatrical

187

with the 'S' sound when you say the words. Listen. There might be a feeling, an attitude, that is stirred within you just from keying in on the repetition of a sound.

In *The Tragedie of Julius Cæsar*, there is the conspiracy scene where Cæsar's assassination is planned. There are sections of verse in which you can hear a preponderance of Ss. For instance Cassius greets and introduces the conspirators to Brutus and says:

> Cassius: This, Decius Brutus.
> Brutus: He is welcome too.
> Cassius: This, Caska; this, Cinna; and this,
> Metellus Cymber[5]

If you count the number of 's' sounds (including the letter 'c' when it is to be pronounced as an 's'), you have eleven Ss alliterating in just three short lines of verse. Now say Cassius's lines aloud. Choose the 's' sound. Not the letter, the sound. See what happens. If you don't notice it yet, give yourself a good acting reason, a JUSTIFICATION if you will, to point up the 's' sound. Is this Shakespeare's way of creating the conspiracy aurally? Can you close your eyes and imagine a group of men whispering about murder? What consonants might prevail? Again in the same section we hear Caska say:

> Caska: You shall confe<u>ss</u>e, that you are both
> de<u>c</u>eiv'd:
> Heere, as I point my <u>S</u>word, the <u>S</u>unne
> arises,
> Which is a great way of growing on the
> <u>S</u>outh,
> Weighing the youthfull <u>S</u>eason of the
> yeare.

Although that singled out passage happened to have six 's' sounds, it is not important or suggested that you count these sounds, whatever the alliterative letter might be. It is important to be aware of them, to notice them. Then again ask your character to choose these sounds by saying them out loud. Listen to what happens.

---

[5] The spellings and punctuation quoted from Shakespeare are those used in the First Folio of 1623.

Don't think about what it means. Just speak. Give up trying to act the words. Let the words act you!

In the example from the First Folio above, you may wonder why certain odd words are capitalized. Words like Sword, Sunne, and Season. It was a printing convention we find in books printed in England and America as recently as the early nineteenth century. For our purposes it is useful to also choose any capitalized letter that seems unusual. Remember, actors would have been the only people reading the lines. Words could have been emphasized for an acting reason.

When you 'choose' any of these verbal conceits, it doesn't necessarily mean you stress or emphasize the word, although that certainly is one way. You can also say the word softer or louder. You can say it faster or slower. You can add a PAUSE before or after the chosen word. You can do as your creativity dictates—then try it out, by MOTIVATING the choice that is giving you a good acting reason.

The same technique applies to **assonance** (same sounding vowels). In *Romeo and Juliet*, the apothecary gives Romeo instructions for using the poison:

Appothecarie:

> Put this in any liquid thing you will
> And drinke it off, and if you hadthe strength
> Of twenty men, it would dispatch you straight.

What clues do you find in the text? Look specifically for words that assonate with one another. In this case choose the 'ihh' sound, as in 'it', 'is' or 'in'. As in listen:

> Put this in any liquid thing you will
> And drinke it off, and if you had the strength
> Of twenty men, it would dispatch you straight.

If you didn't hear it, say the above three lines again and really exaggerate the 'ihh's'. In fact build on them. Make each one stronger than the next. Don't be afraid to go OVER THE TOP.

Look at all those 'ihh' sounds. What about 'em? What do they really mean? Perhaps not a thing. But to reiterate, choose them and say them aloud. Verse technique doesn't work by doing it in your head. See what you can use theatrically. There is no right or wrong way. There is only what works on the stage and what doesn't. Can you picture an old apothecary or druggist of the time handing the poison to Romeo and going, "ihh, ihh, ihh, ihh, ihh!" while he squints and rubs his hands together as if cleansing away his conspiratorial actions. That is only one proposed attitude you might try with the above clue. It's very theatrical and it tells the story. What choices will you make?

Let's take a look at **sexual innuendo**. Of the many ways of using words to manipulate you, entice you, and command your attention, sex is the most efficient, the most penetrating (pun intended), and the most fun. Shakespeare was a wordsmith. As actors your job is to find the sexual innuendo and use it as Shakespeare's direction.

Let's look at Juliet's speech in Act three, scene two. The SOLILOQUY begins:

> Gallop apace, you fiery footed steedes,
> Towards *Phebus* lodging, such a Wagoner
> As *Phaeton* would whip you to the west,
> And bring in Cloudie night immediately.

The speech moves on to:

> And learne me how to loose a winning match,
> Plaid for a paire of stainlesse Maidenhoods,
> Hood my unman'd blood bayting in my Cheekes,
> With thy Blacke mantle, till strange Love grow
>   bold,
> Thinke true Love acted simple modestie:
> Come night, come *Romeo*, come thou day in
>   night,
> For thou wilt lie upon the wings of night
> Whiter then new Snow upon a Raven's backe:
> Come gentle night, come loving blackebrow'd
>   night.

Steamy stuff. First a play on words with lose and win (loose a winning match). Then another play on words with maidenhoods and hood (Plaid for a paire of stainlesse Maiden*hoods*, *Hood* my unman'd blood bayting in my Cheekes). In the next line you have, "till strange

Love grow bold." Quick! What else besides "love" might "grow bold".

Now we come to the 'comes'. At the end of the section we have the word 'come' repeated five times. What do you think that's about? Most of you are right. Some of you may not want to know. And who really knows for sure? The answer is in the way it plays for an audience. Eric Partridge,[6] the English scholar and lexicographer says in *Shakespeare's Bawdy* that 'come' means, "To experience a sexual emission." That's his learned opinion. Some things however seem theatrically obvious. Take Hamlet and Ophelia in Act three, scene two:

Queen:	Come hither my good *Hamlet*, sit by me.
Hamlet:	No good Mother, Here's Mettle[7] more attractive.
Polonius:	Oh ho, do you marke that?
Hamlet:	Ladie, shall I llye in your Lap?
Ophelia:	No my Lord.
Hamlet:	I mean, my Head upon your Lap?
Ophelia:	I my Lord.
Hamlet:	Do you think I meant Country matters?
Ophelia:	I thinke nothing, my Lord.
Hamlet:	That's a faire thought to ly between Maids legs

What matters do you think Hamlet meant? And if we take a directorial *cue* from Shakespeare and "Suite the Action to the Word, the Word to the Action," might Hamlet's head be aimed at Ophelia's... lap? And if that's so, what comes to mind when he says Country matters. Can you see (or hear would be more accurate) that this is a reference to sexual matters? What do you hear in the word 'Country'? In any case, sexual innuendo is where you find it. So look for it and play (with) it.

When we look at the Folio for **spelling** and punctuation, we can again draw certain directorial inferences.

---

[6] *Shakespeare's Bawdy*, by Eric Partridge (New York: E. P. Dutton & Co., Inc., 1969). Mr. Partridge is a world authority on slang and colloquial English. His *Dictionary of Slang and Unconventional English* (1937) is a standard classic in its field.

[7] Could be short for mettlesome or spunky according to Partridge, courageous, high spirited meaning 'sexually vigorous or ardent'.

Elizabethans spelled phonetically. They spelled words as they heard them. You will often see the same word spelled differently within the same page. In *Love's Labours Lost*, Costard says, "Mee?" then "Me?" then "Still mee?" ending with "O me." The directorial note then is to say the word the way it's written and discover what the LINE READING might have been. Also the word 'oh' is spelled two ways. 'Oh' and 'O'. 'Oh' is regular, and 'O' demands a full commitment. These distinctions and 'clues' unfortunately have been edited out of the popular editions. They are only in the Folio.

Punctuation also gives you clues. If you give an actor a line ending in an **exclamation point**, you are giving an emotional interpretation and directing the actor to play it as such. Shakespeare used exclamation points sparingly. Editors use them a lot! Often an editor will interpret a scene based on his scholarship and his opinion of what the scene is about. Editors will often claim that the verse in the First Folio is faulty, sloppy or otherwise filled with errors. The editors then regularize the line, as Dr. Flatter points out, to make the verse neater. Unfortunately the scene no longer plays the same way. When actors work from the text in the Folio, the closest thing we have to what Shakespeare wrote, the scene is always more interesting, understandable, and dramatic.

In order to acknowledge the verse, you need to acknowledge the end of a line. It's the punctuation that tells you how best to handle the end of each line. In verse know that a **period, question mark** or an exclamation point not only signals the end of a sentence but the end of a thought as well. When you come to a period, drop your voice. Allow the listener's ear to relax and absorb what you've just said. A **comma** means a continuation of the thought. When you arrive at a comma, lift your voice. It will hold the listener's attention. Example: *As You Like It*, Act two, scene one:

> *Celia*: With his eies full of anger.
> [Period. End thought. Drop your voice.]
> *Duke*: Mistris, dispatch you with your safest haste,
> [Comma. Continue thought. Lift your voice.]
> And get you from the Court.
> [Period. End thought. Drop your voice.]

The point here is to acknowledge the verse by 'choosing' the end of the line, regardless of punctuation. Not to preserve the integrity of the line for verse sake, but because the verse structure is our clue to direction. Discover for yourself, through the verse, what your character is doing. When you see a **colon** or a **semi-colon** know your thought isn't finished. If it's a semi-colon, treat the thought as if you were adding an imaginary 'and'. When you're confronted with a colon, it's as if you're saying 'but' or 'as well as', as a way of continuing the thought. Find a theatrical way to hold the audience's attention through all the parts of a whole thought. A change in rhythm is helpful for a start. **Parentheses** also indicate a GEAR CHANGE.

Speaking of each line of verse or **lineage**, let's examine a few clues revealed in the way the lines of verse are structured. If you have a perfect line of **iambic pentameter**, that is, five metric feet to the line, you have a strong **masculine** ending. If, as often happens, you have a line with eleven beats, the extra syllable makes you stress the second to the last syllable, thereby weakening the line. It's called a **feminine** ending. These verse rules were obviously worked out before Women's Lib. If you count twelve beats to the line it's an **alexandrine**, the natural meter of the French. The directorial note is that you're trying to load more thought into the line than the line will hold. Ask your character to do the same in the way you say it.

An **incomplete line** or a **half-line** usually indicates a pause for stage business. If there are two half-lines, one after the other, it's Shakespeare's way of telling the second actor to come in on CUE. And a **mid-line ending** is also the playwright asking you to come in one cue.

There is one clear disadvantage to verse. Because it's written line by line, actors have a tendency to stop at the end of a line regardless of where the thought ends. It's called **end-stopping**. Carry the thought straight on through to the end of the sentence, finding a theatrical way of acknowledging each line as you go.

Obviously you can't learn verse technique, or acting for that matter, from a book. The original actors performing in Shakespeare's company would have begun their careers as apprentices. They would have been taught to read and schooled in verse and stage techniques by the journeymen actors they served. They would have spent years learning and practicing their CRAFT by doing it. This section is intended to give you some alternative choices in preparing your verse roles. It is a skill and like any other skill needs practice.

Also, it is not expected that you will be cast in a play in which actors are given their parts on scrolls with no rehearsal. What we can learn from this is the way that Shakespeare's actors might have worked on their parts. For if the plays were written with the foreknowledge of how they would be acted, and Shakespeare was an actor, then it makes sense to begin our EXPLORATION of the part where Shakespeare left off.

When you read about a technique such as this, it may seem at first to be mechanical and artificial. When you play the scenes this way you feel what it's like for Shakespeare to put you in the same position as the character. The behavior is very truthful and compelling.

METHOD trained actors, who work from the inside out, may rebel against this way of working because it approaches a part from the outside in. As long as we arrive at the middle, as long as we gain entrance to the house, what's the difference whether we come in through the front door or the back door. This is not the 'right' way or the 'wrong' way, it is simply 'a' way. Give it a try. Experiment with your own way of using these ideas. Keep in mind that Shakespeare's men would be able to see these clues immediately without employing a technique. Their verse technique would have been absorbed by the time they played in public. So must your technique be absorbed. No one wants to see the work. Once these ideas are repeated enough they will become second nature. Only then will you be well versed in verse.

In the words of T. S. Eliot, "About anyone so great as Shakespeare it is probable that we can never be right; and if we can never be right, it is better that we should from time to time change our way of being wrong."

Vulnerability

The actor's ability to process various stimuli and express the response in the moment. Allowing outside elements in, to touch your pain, and release the result.

Vulnerability is power! Many actors don't know that. It is vital for actors to understand and use this essential point. No one likes to experience PAIN and discomfort. There seems to be a natural tendency to associate being vulnerable with being weak. It ain't so in theatre, and it ain't so in life.

In the 1930s a new comic strip character emerged called Superman. Superman was a big hit, but there was one major problem for the strip's survival. Superman was invulnerable. Nothing could harm the man of steel. Since nothing or no one could hurt him, people began not to care. Superman's invulnerability nearly killed him.[1]

The creators of the Superman comic strip, in order to save Superman and the strip, created kryptonite, the only element that could harm Superman. They created Superman's vulnerability in order to make him stronger. In order for him to survive.

New actors need to understand and develop their ability to express their vulnerability. Sometimes it seems as though the actor is invulnerable. This is just the actor's cover. He's developed that cover over many years as a survival mechanism. When the actor begins to understand that the only way to do what he wants to do on stage to another actor requires vulnerability, then he works toward releasing the vulnerability that is already in him.

Dana was a young actress who was as tough as they come. She was nineteen. She had a survival job through a member of her family that allowed her to be boss to several employees and earn a lot of money for her age.

In class Dana did an IMPROV to help her deal with her vulnerability. She was put on stage with another actor named Dennis. It was explained to her how difficult a process it is to fire someone and deny him his livelihood. "Dana", said the director, "I want you to fire Dennis for being late for the third time". The improv took about a minute. After Dennis was ushered into the 'office', Dana said, "Look Dennis, I've told you about being late three times and you don't listen. That's it! You're fired! I want you out of here immediately!" Then she looked up at us and smiled. She felt she was fast, thorough, and successful with the improv. In short, that meant she was a good actor.

---

[1] As this book went to press Superman was killed. His creators are planning to bring him back to life.

Vulnerability

It was explained to her that the improv was set up as a means of working on her vulnerability, or lack of it. She was told, among other things, that the improv wasn't believable. She had braced herself and followed her INTENTION no matter what, with no give and take. She slowly began to understand the need for vulnerability in order to be 'correct' with her work.

Several classes later we were doing an exercise designed for actors to deal with vulnerability in scenes. It's called 'please come to my side of the stage.' Two actors are asked to stand on either side of the stage. Each has to get the other to come to his side of the stage. They're not allowed to get physical and drag their partners over to them. They're even told going into the exercise that the key is vulnerability.

We had done the exercise with several actors (it usually takes many attempts over the course of weeks or months to succeed in the exercise). Things were going well. Then Dana got on stage with Dennis. There was also one actor who had no partner (there was an odd number of actors that day). Her name was Millie and she tended to be overbearing and insensitive to others. Dana was told, "You're so tough that we're going to ask Millie to stand STAGE LEFT with Dennis, and it will be two against one. You have to get both of them over to your side of the stage." Now Dennis and Dana were close friends outside of class and we could see that Dana was disturbed. Millie whispered into Dennis's ear some strategy in a catty conspiratorial way. Dana got jealous and really hurt. We saw Dana about to drop the atomic bomb on both of them. The director yelled "freeze!" Dana was reminded to let her feelings and impulses express themselves, that the key to 'winning' was vulnerability. All of a sudden she did it. She let the hurt in. Then she expressed it. She looked at Dennis. She was totally herself and she simply and eloquently said, "Dennis you can't believe how much your whispering to each other hurts me. I feel alone and I feel scared (there were tears in her eyes now). Would you please hug me? I need you."

Without missing a beat Dennis was compelled to walk over to Dana and give her the hug she earned. It was a BREAKTHROUGH in her work. Then this happened. Millie was still standing there, alone and somewhat unsure of what to do. Dana looked at her and, just by expressing the vulnerability that was there, melted away

Millie's coarseness and invulnerability by saying to her, "It feels awful doesn't it?" Millie nodded yes. Dana said, "Come on over and give us both a hug." Millie did, and everybody won, Dana, Dennis, Millie, and the class. Game, set, and match. It was a graphic demonstration of 'vulnerability is power'.

What If (as opposed to, or in addition to As If)

Not an official term, but an important creative question to be a part of any artist's craft.

In the early 1900s STANISLAVSKI trained the actor's believ-ability by using a technique called AS IF. Enter your house as if you are entering a palace, he would say, etc. 'As if' has entered the CRAFT of most actors even if they were not aware of Stanislavski's formal term.

Today one of the most important questions an actor can ask is, "What if?" The instant you've decided on a cre-ative CHOICE to try in REHEARSAL or PREPARATION, perform the choice but don't let the questions end there? Keep your IMAGINATION going. Ask what if? Then try it by playing it.

Every time you ask 'what if' you are employing a ve-hicle that will take you further into the depths of creativity. It's when you stop questioning that you stop creating.

When you're in performance, after your choices have been assimilated and rehearsed, continue to ask 'what if'. I don't mean that you should do something you didn't rehearse and throw off your partner or your direc-tor, but you can still question other ways to achieve your OBJECTIVE.

Asking 'what if' is only half the job, the other half is turning it into ACTION by doing it. Any time you employ 'what if', make sure you keep it in the present. If you let the statement address the past, you will be dealing with a negative choice. 'What if' is not at all the same as 'if only'. 'What if' means suppose I try this, or do this, or think this, or touch this. 'What if' is a never ending choice of action. 'What if' is a way to keep yourself curious, in a state of wonder. When you are curious you become fascinated and fascinating. Infants and children are in a continuous state of wonder. That is part of their innate ability to make believe. Fill yourself with wonder. Your acting will be wonderful.

Afterword

People buy books on acting because they're looking for answers. You can view the preceding pages as a collection of answers and perhaps derive some short-term gain. This endeavor however was to provide the stimulus to ask the 'right' questions.

Any good class or teacher can teach you acting techniques in six months. It is hoped that the terms, techniques, and ideas contained herein become a vessel, a vehicle to tap into the soul and gain access to the spirit.

It is our job as artists to express the light and the darkness residing in our own souls and so touch an audience, individuals, each of whom is an artist within himself. For a soul to touch another soul, that is the result. Art, any art, is merely the process that transports us there. To paraphrase Camus, "If man understood the enigmas of life, there would be no need for the arts."

Bibliography and Reading List

Aaron, Stephen, *Stage Fright* (Chicago: University of
　　　Chicago Press, 1986)
Adler, Stella, *Technique of Acting, The* (New York:
　　　Bantam Books, 1988)
Barton, John, *Playing Shakespeare* (London: Methuen
　　　Ltd., 1984, New York: Methuen Inc., 1984)
Boleslavski, Richard, *ACTING, the First Six Lessons*
　　　(New York: Theatre Arts Books, 1933)
Checkhov, Anton, *Selected Letters of Anton Chekhov*
　　　(New York: Farrar, Strauss, Giroux, 1955)
Chekhov, Michael, *To the Actor* (New York: Harper and
　　　Row, Inc., 1953)
Clurman, Harold, *Harold Clurman on Directing* (London:
　　　Collier Macmillan, 1972)
Cole, Toby, *Acting, a Handbook of the Stanislavski Method*
　　　(New York: Crown Publishing, 1947)
Cole, Toby, and Helen Krich Chinoy, eds., *Actors on
　　　Acting* (New York: Crown Publishing, 1954)
Easty, Edward Dwight, *On Method Acting* (Florida:
　　　House of Collectibles, Inc., 1966)
Flatter, Richard, *Shakespeare's Producing Hand* (New
　　　York: W.W. Norton & Co., 1948)
Gorchakov, Nikolai, *Vakhtangov School of Stage Art, The*
　　　Moscow Foreign Language Publishing House,
　　　1961)
Gordon, Mel, *Stanislavsky Technique, The* (New York:
　　　Applause Theatre Book Publishers, 1987)
Gurr, Andrew, *Shakespearean Stage, The* (Cambridge,
　　　England: Cambridge University Press, 1980)
Hagan, Uta, and Haskel Frankel, *Respect for Acting* (New
　　　York: Macmillan Co., 1973)
Hinman, Charlton, *First Folio of Shakespeare (Norton
　　　Facsimile), The* (New York: W.W. Norton & Co.,
　　　1968)
Holland, James and B.F. Skinner, *Analysis of Behavior,
　　　The* (New York: McGraw-Hill, 1961)
Lewis, Robert, *Method or Madness* (New York: Samuel
　　　French, Inc., 1958)
Magarshack, David, *Stanislavsky, on the Art of the Stage*
　　　(Winchester, MA: Faber & Faber, Inc., 1950)
Meisner, S. and P. Longwell, *Sanford Meisner on Acting*
　　　(New York: Vintage Books, 1987)

Partridge, Eric, *Shakespeare's Bawdy* (New York: E.P. Dutton & Co., Inc., 1969)

Rubinstein, Frankie, *Dictionary of Shakespeare's Sexual Puns and Their Significance* (London: The Macmillan Press, Ltd., 1984

Russell, John and Vonie Morrison, *Act Naturally* (Bakersfield, CA: Blue Book Music, 1963–1971)

Rutter, Carol, *Documents of the Rose Playhouse* (Cambridge, England: Cambridge University Press, 1984)

Shurtleff, Michael, *Audition* (New York: Walker and Company, 1978)

Stanislavsky, Constantin, *An Actor Prepares* (New York: Theatre Arts Books, 1936)

———— *Building a Character* (New York: Theatre Arts Books, 1949)

———— *Creating a Role* (New York: Theatre Arts Books, 1961)

———— *My Life in Art* (New York: Routledge/Theatre Arts, 1924)

Strasberg, Lee, *Dream of Passion, A* (Boston: Little Brown and Company, 1987)

Strasberg, Lee and Robert Hethmon, *Strasberg at the Actors Studio* (New York: Viking Press, 1965)

About the Author

Doug Moston has been working in theatre for over twenty-five years. In 1965 he began his career as an actor, studying with such noted teachers as William Hickey, Warren Robertson, Arthur Storch, Kim Stanley, Ernie Martin, and Herbert Berghof, and was an observer at The Actors Studio under Harold Clurman and Lee Strasberg. He worked professionally in theatre, film, and television until 1979 when he began teaching and directing. He has lectured at Queens College, taught at several institutions including The American Academy of Dramatic Arts and, most recently, The Actors Studio. Over the last ten years he has worked with various theatre companies such as The Off-Center Theatre and Riverside Shakespeare Company, in charge of selecting and directing original and classical plays. Mr. Moston currently teaches acting in New York where he is Artistic Director of Drama Project, a not-for-profit company of actors, playwrights and directors working together to develop new plays. He is a member director of the Playwrights/Directors Unit of The Actors Studio and serves on the Blue Ribbon Panel of the National Academy of Television Arts and Sciences which selects best actor, director and show for the Emmy Awards. He is also a columnist for the show business newspaper <u>Actors Resource</u>. Mr. Moston is a member of Actors' Equity Association, Screen Actors Guild and the American Federation of Radio and Television Artists.